OUR TURN

Our

To Dearest Ismé –
This book – This life –
would not have been possible
without you !

KIRSTINE STEWART

Turn

 Random House Canada

PUBLISHED BY RANDOM HOUSE CANADA

Published in 2015 by Random House Canada, a division of
Penguin Random House Canada Limited. Distributed in Canada
by Penguin Random House Canada Limited, Toronto.

www.penguinrandomhouse.ca

Library and Archives Canada Cataloguing in Publication

Stewart, Kirstine
Our turn / Kirstine Stewart.

Issued in print and electronic formats.

ISBN 978-0-345-81463-0
eBook ISBN 978-0-345-81465-4

1. Stewart, Kirstine. 2. Women executives.
3. Leadership in women. 4. Women in television broadcasting.
I. Title.

HD6054.3.S789 2015   658.4'0920825   C2015-903825-1

Book design by CS Richardson

Cover image: © Markian Lozowchuk

Printed and bound in the United States of America

2 4 6 8 9 7 5 3 1

Penguin
Random House
RANDOM HOUSE CANADA

To family:
the one I was grateful to be born into
and the one I was lucky to find along the way.

[CONTENTS]

Girl Friday Rises

WE HEAR AND READ almost daily about the conspicuous absence of women from the highest echelons of corporations, companies and countries. Women outnumber men as university graduates, enter the workforce in roughly equal numbers as men do, yet the further up the ladder you look, the fewer women you find. A recent study from Catalyst, the non-profit research group focused on women in the workplace, revealed that women in Canada hold just 18 percent of senior officer jobs and 36 percent of management positions. Among Fortune 500 companies, women occupy only 17 percent of board seats, 14 percent of executive positions, and make up less than 5 percent of chief executive officers. Data like this are splintering the woman's movement—think Sheryl Sandberg's *Lean In* versus Anne-Marie Slaughter's "Why Women Still Can't Have It All."

Much of the debate seems to swirl like a sandstorm around an insidious riddle: What comes first, having more women at the top in order to create change or making change so that women can reach the top?

I believe it's time we look at the conundrum differently. It's time to stop agonizing over how to affect change and to exploit the reality that profound *change* is already under way, a revolution in fact. Fuelled by technology and shifting demographics, digital technologies are creating a new world order that demands a new style of leader—one with attributes and perspectives that make women natural front-runners. That's not just my view. That's the conclusion from a growing body of research that finds women tend to have in spades what's needed to lead successfully in the information age. It really is "our turn." The question now, and one I hope to answer in these pages, is how best do we seize it?

Having worked my way up from the bottom, without the benefit of an Ivy League education or friends in high places, it's a question I'm regularly asked. And having worked under a long list of leaders, men and women, good and bad, it's also one I feel I can answer by sharing the hard-won lessons of my own experience. Our culture is steeped in the narrative of the self-made man; the stories of self-made women are relatively new and still unfolding, mine included. But I've seen enough from the front lines of power to understand the forces that are now redefining it. My experience has given me a unique perspective on what it takes to lead and to get ahead in our changing world, if that's what you choose to do.

IN MY CASE, getting ahead was a necessity as much as a choice. It was back in 1988. I had big hair, rent to pay on my first apartment and (long before my career moves made headlines) a newspaper was a place I scoured to *find* a job. Of course, the bottom of the heap was not exactly what I had pictured for myself. After graduating with an English literature degree, I had imagined an auspicious career launch in publishing. I even had a position lined up with the publishing house where I'd interned. But then the recession hit, the job disappeared and I was desperate, not only to cover the bills, but to start my "real life"—somewhere, anywhere. So when I saw the ad for a "girl Friday" placed by a television company in the classified section of the *Toronto Star*, I applied.

The term didn't even strike me as sexist, just quaint, a throwback to the other end of the century, circa typing pools and steno pads. I read it as a call for a junior assistant willing to do anything and everything, which wasn't much different from the varied jobs I'd been juggling to put myself through university. I had worked as a cashier at a bookshop and a discount department store. I'd filed reference materials at the university library, and, at the agricultural museum near where I'd grown up, I played the part of an 1860s farm wife for three summers. Sporting a bonnet and petticoats, I churned butter, baked bread, tacked quilts, spun cotton and carded wool. Playing girl Friday sounded pretty easy by comparison.

I told myself I'd find my way into publishing eventually, and, in the meantime, getting a foot in the door of a television company was an interesting alternative. I'd never thought about jobs in TV. I'm not sure I realized working in TV was even a possibility. To me, TV was a pastime, though when I was a kid, it had been an addiction. *The Flintstones* and *Bewitched* repeats, *Mork & Mindy*, *Family Ties*—my parents apparently never worried too much TV would rot my brain.

I'd skipped grades in elementary school and they actually credited *Sesame Street* for giving me a preschool head start (and keeping me occupied). Now, here was an unexpected opportunity to look behind the scenes.

Paragon Entertainment, which produced and sold television programs to broadcasters around the world, hired me as their girl Friday straight out of school. I landed in the small downtown office of its distribution wing, Paragon International, where a handful of sales executives pitched a popular homegrown lineup, such as the tween drama *Degrassi*, an animated kids' series called *The Raccoons*, and *Monster Truck* (yes, it was an action series starring those bouncing, supersized monster pick-ups). I ran errands, ordered office supplies, and handled the mail, the phones, telexes, faxes and photocopies. In the process, I got my head around the business, all of which was run by one formidable woman.

"Oh, you have a *female* boss?" my mother said when she heard. "That's not always a good thing."

MY MOTHER WAS BORN in a man's world—a small English industrial town during the Second World War. Still, as the youngest of five children in a lower-middle-class family, she grew up believing that a woman should be prepared to pay her own way. A talented artist, she became a draftsperson for architectural firms where usually she was one of very few women at the table. In those days, the rare woman who did manage to acquire a piece of the leadership pie was often loath to share even a crumb with another woman working her way up. When there wasn't enough to go around, another woman was the competition.

Even today, surveys find that women—even more than males—would rather work for a man than another woman. Gallup has tracked the gender preference for a male-over-female boss since the 1950s, and while it has narrowed over time, it hasn't disappeared. It may be that women's ongoing insecurities in the workplace have carried through the decades, making female bosses tougher on other women. Or it may be that powerful women tend to be perceived as cold and controlling as they vie for a seat at what had traditionally been a man's table. Or it may be that people don't want to work for their mothers. Whatever sparks it, society tends to view the gender preference as further evidence that women's bid for equality in the workplace, specifically success at the highest levels, has faltered.

I certainly took my mother's concerns to heart at the time. But I also kept an open mind. Luckily, fate had put me under the wing of Isme Bennie. She was Paragon's president and someone I actually would come to regard, professionally, as my second mother. Not that there was any coddling from Isme. It wasn't her style.

A self-made woman who worked her way up and out of her hometown in South Africa, Isme had a powerful, colourful presence. Fashionable and worldly, she knew the business better than anyone. As a boss, she was exacting, ferocious—*The Devil Wears Prada*, but without the horns. Demanding, yes, but never, ever mean. Isme was reserved with her praise, but if she saw something she liked, she rewarded it. I'd been there six months when I got my first promotion. I found a letter sitting in an envelope on my desk one morning that informed me that along with an annual salary bump from

$16,000 to $18,000, I had been promoted from girl Friday to sales executive with one stroke of her pen.

Isme later explained that she'd heard me on the phone, where instead of taking messages, I took initiative. I asked broadcasters what they were looking for and described the shows that might be a good fit. "It makes sense for you to be a sales executive," she said. "You're already doing the job."

With that promotion came the freedom to rise and shine. I travelled with her to international film and television festivals in Cannes and Monte Carlo, cutting deals with TV networks from around the world. After the Iron Curtain fell, I sold the first Western show into Russia, our kids' show, *The Raccoons,* in exchange for bolts of fabric, which, unlike Russian currency at the time, could be converted into cash through a Montreal textile company. I rose to become a sales manager in charge of business in the Middle East, South East Asia and Africa. When the publishing firm where I'd interned finally did call to offer me the job I'd once pined for, I turned them down. I had fallen completely for the media world I'd stumbled into, its unique mix of business and content creation, commerce and art.

When Isme left Paragon in 1995 to run Bravo, a new arts specialty channel, I replaced her. In seven years, and before I turned 30, I'd gone from girl Friday to president of a multi-million-dollar television distribution company.

I'VE BEEN FORTUNATE. The professional trajectory of those early years has become the pattern of my career in media, now closing in on three decades. I've headed up programming at two American networks, run a large group of

Canadian channels at Alliance Atlantis, including Home and Garden Television (HGTV), and, in 2006, I was tapped to take over television at the Canadian Broadcasting Corporation (CBC). Four years later, I was promoted to what many consider the top of the broadcast food chain in Canada, executive vice-president over the entire operation of the CBC's English Language Services, becoming, at forty-two, the youngest person to hold the job, and the first woman.

Ever since, in interviews and at talks I give, people ask me how I did it, how I managed to climb high up the corporate ladder without old money or connections. Successful men are seldom asked the same question, and rarely are they subjected to the level of scrutiny women receive when they arrive in the C-suite. For a woman, there's always the lurking thought that she's had some help in beating the odds, particularly if she ascends to an office no woman has occupied before. Especially when she's a relatively young woman, who also happens to be a mother of two, as I am.

That set of largely unvoiced suspicions haunted me through my tenure at the CBC. They also haunted me when I decided to leave the job in 2013 to become the first head of Twitter Canada, a move the national press trumpeted as a front-page surprise and put under a microscope. After all, given that during my time at the helm of CBC we had commissioned hits like *Dragon's Den* and *Little Mosque on the Prairie*, and won back the rights to the Olympics, I'd overseen one of the most successful periods in the public broadcaster's seventy-five-year history, in terms of ratings, revenues and, for a while, even morale. And yet, I was bolting. How could I leave one of the most powerful jobs in Canadian media, a major position many women, and men, would kill to have, and to keep? I felt a twinge of guilt that I was somehow letting my gender down: I'd broken through a thick glass ceiling at a venerable old institution only to walk away from the shards.

No man had ever quit the CBC's top job. They were either fired or they retired. I was jumping from being chief executive of a coast-to-coast radio and television operation of 5,000 employees to an empty office—no colleagues, no employees, no assistant, just me and a smartphone, a pioneer on the tech frontier (no bonnet or spinning wheel). I could see how it seemed slightly absurd.

Yet I believe my decision to resign was one of the boldest and smartest career moves I have ever made. In the first year after I took the post, Twitter became a publicly traded company and one of the most valuable in the world with a valuation of US$29 billion. I led the Twitter Canada team to a banner launch that multiplied revenues, made the country a major priority for the company and led to my next opportunity at Twitter HQ. Since the fall of 2014, after Twitter asked if I would take on a bigger job as VP of Media, I've been heading up all our news, sports, entertainment and government-related content and activities for our partners across North America—from coverage of the Super Bowl to the Oscars, to the launch of Hillary Clinton's presidential campaign. I haven't slipped into the obscurity of the corporate wild. I'm playing in a wide-open field that's dramatically changing the way the world shares and communicates. So now, when people ask for tips from my own path to success, I tell them this: My leap from the top ranks of old media to the new is emblematic of a much larger transition, one that should give women, especially, every reason to be optimistic about their futures.

No corner of society—public, private, economic or political—has been untouched by the warp-speed proliferation of technology. Barely two decades into the twenty-first century, it's transferring power from organizations to people, remaking institutions, transforming industries, spawning coups (the Arab Spring's netizens), electing presidents (#AskObama) and altering forever the way we do business. No company can afford not to change. Consider the corporate giants that have fallen in the last two decades alone: Kodak, Nokia, Blockbuster Video, Tower Records and Borders. Once one of the largest bookstore chains in the US, Borders made the critical mistake of failing to embrace e-commerce; it did not invest in the development of its own e-reader and over-invested in music at a time when people stopped buying CDs and started buying iPods. It closed the doors on its remaining stores in 2011. Companies that fail to respond quickly to the new appetites and realities of the consumer-driven market simply fail themselves. Between 2010 and 2011, that toll included more than three hundred American newspapers that folded for good.

At the same time, the digital age is proving that big is not necessarily better in the business world. With ready access to big data, companies are getting smaller. The Swedish company Mojang AB, creators of Minecraft, the best-selling PC video game to date, only has 40 employees. In 2013, it generated $292 million in revenues and in November 2014 was snapped up by Microsoft for a reported $2.5 billion. BuzzFeed, the online news site that's giving media old and new a run for its money, has about 700 employees and pulled in a reported $100 million in revenue last year. Netflix, which describes itself as the "world's leading Internet television provider," accounting for 30 percent of downstream traffic during peak hours in North America, generated more than $4.3 billion in revenue in 2013, and has just 2,000 employees. That's one-tenth the number of employees at CBS. Size is no longer an indicator of success. And neither are assets. Uber, the world's biggest taxi company, has no taxis. Airbnb, poised to become the world's largest hotelier, has no hotels. Amazon, the on-line retail giant that has put countless book and music stores out of business, has no stores.

The knowledge economy is upending business models. Hierarchical, bureaucratic management structures are dying and traditional leadership profiles are dying with them. Gone are the days where rigid leaders who issue edicts from on high through layers of management can expect the world to go their way. Now the world has a say. With the reach of social media, and the staggering volume of credible data available online 24/7 about customers, products and the competition, today's leaders must be keen listeners, responsive and flexible. They can't rely on being the smartest one in the room with all the answers—the Internet gives everyone answers. The new effective leaders are those with the long-term vision to ask the right questions. They lead teams, not staff. They foster networks, not silos, creating a culture in which everyone collaborates and multi-tasking is as instinctive as breathing.

So many of the qualities essential to modern leadership— anticipating events and the needs of others, listening, collaborating, multi-tasking, being flexible—are the very same characteristics that for so long cast women in the role of valued assistants, those quintessential girl Fridays. Of course, opportunity is ripe not just for women, but for anyone who wants to lead differently. (As it happens, the original "girl Friday" was actually a man, the fictional sidekick of Robinson Crusoe, prized for his loyalty and ability to take on any task.)

Revolutions never happen in isolation. Most of history's major social shifts have come on the heels of other seismic events: the industrial revolution fuelled the growth of cities and of sickness, too, and the concept of public health was born; the Second World War brought women to the workplace en masse and sparked the second wave of feminism. Today, the digital revolution is not the only force reshaping leadership. On the horizon, a demographic eruption is about to play its own dazzling role.

As the population ages, and old boys' clubs with it, the largest population cohort since the Baby Boom is entering the workforce with values, attitudes and expectations never seen before. Born between 1980 and 2000, the Millennials, also known as Generation Y, are projected to account for 50 percent of the workforce by 2020 and 75 percent by 2025. Companies around the world are scrambling to figure out how this new breed of worker will fit within their corporate structures. Millennials, after all, are digital natives, the first generation to reach the workplace having grown up with personal computers, smartphones, tablets and rich social media networks. They're the engine driving the revolution, and new branches of research devoted to figuring them out. Studies find them to be liberal, well educated, racially diverse and disdainful of traditional top-down authority. If predictions are right, they're poised to downsize and dismantle cubicles and corner offices wherever they find them.

At the same time, the women of Generation Y are emerging as an exciting cohort within a cohort. These young women are more likely than any other females in history to have grown up with a working mother as a role model. While women of previous generations have been far less likely than their male peers to say they intend to pursue leadership roles, a 2014 research paper from the Pew Center has found that Millennial women have higher aspirations to become bosses, or managers, than females of any other age group.

Both my daughters are Millennials. My eldest, born the year after I became president of Paragon, is about to make her way in the world with the refreshing sense that nothing is beyond her reach. And her expectations are high. When she was about ten, she learned that I was named one of Canada's "Top 40 Under 40" and her question was, "Well, what number *are* you?" What I tell her about ambition, as I would tell any woman, is that success is not just about climbing. Leading comes from learning, in all its forms, and personal happiness will only be yours when you choose your own ladder.

In the fraught discussions about the dearth of women in leadership roles, there's been too much focus on reaching the top. Altitude is not the only measure of success. You can choose to be a leader in whatever work you do, at whatever level, because "leadership" is a mindset. It's how you work: how you learn to grow and spend your personal capital. That mindset can be applied to whatever endeavour you undertake, wherever you choose to invest yourself, or whatever circumstances your life allows. Struggling to make ends meet rarely affords a woman the freedom to pursue ambitions, which, after desperation led me to the classifieds, was the first professional lesson I learned. Still, what you do with what you have can turn tides, whether you're a girl Friday, lead a Fortune 500 company, a family, a project or yourself. It's time to think and be leaders in life, in all its spheres.

I wrote this book, using the lens of my own continuing adventures in leadership, in order to explore the forces that can not only derail a rise to the top, but those that hold us back from contributing the unique gifts and insights we have to offer whether we hold a traditional leadership position or not. Those forces may be external, but often, as I discovered, they are internal—and as daunting as any glass ceiling.

But now, when the digital revolution has put unprecedented power in the hands of each one of us, the future depends on finding the best way to use it. That's not just good for women, that's good for business, and the world we're remaking.

First, Lead Yourself

IN THE SUMMER OF 2006, I took the stage for my first "upfront" at the CBC. Upfronts are big deals in the television industry, annual events where networks reveal their prime-time schedules for the coming season to generate buzz and pre-sell commercial airtime. That June day, the crowd was thick. Staff, marketers, advertisers and media had all made their way to a cavernous studio on the tenth floor of the CBC building in downtown Toronto, where I was set to unveil a unique new lineup with a whole lot riding on it.

Just four months earlier, I'd joined the CBC as executive director of programming, overseeing drama, comedy, news documentaries and sports. I'd been tasked with the specific mandate of bringing more eyeballs to the network's shows— ideally, millions of pairs. It was a tall order. At the time, the only CBC show that came close to attracting a million viewers was the Saturday night stalwart *Hockey Night in Canada*. But my aims were broader than adding eyeballs. As I saw it, they had to be. The CBC was a media company in desperate need of a makeover, inside and out. For starters, the public broadcaster didn't always see itself as a *media* company, but rather a government-subsidized cultural institution charged with the woolly mission of delivering authoritative news and content. Aside from news programming and *Hockey Night in Canada*, most of its primetime offerings were unable to compete for ratings with big American shows, or even with the homegrown fare featured on the country's private networks. At the same time, its digital content was creaking behind the demand of audiences who increasingly expected shows and information to be available whenever and however they wanted them. The bottom line: the CBC's ties to Canadians as a valued entertainment source were becoming threadbare. It was getting difficult for the people who worked there to see a way out.

So while my mission was to reverse the spiral of falling ratings and revenues, I knew none of that could happen without modernizing the organization and shoring up morale— quickly. I also knew I couldn't do it alone. Without everyone playing hard on the same side, we'd never reach success of any kind. Which is why the first test was mine. No team wants to follow a coach they don't trust, and to many inside the CBC, I was a stranger (and to some, short on credibility). If people—staff and the public—were to believe the public broadcaster could again become meaningful and relevant, there had to be evidence of it in that first lineup of shows I commissioned. If I didn't make a splash, I'd sink.

A Lone Wolf Can't Get There

UNDERSTANDING THE BIG PICTURE and the prize you're playing for is an asset no matter what level you work at, but for anyone who hopes to lead, it's essential. You have to know where you want to end up in order to chart the way forward, whether you're talking about a project or an entire organization. Good leaders have a clear view of the goal, and they're passionate about reaching it. At the CBC, it looked a lot like having to cross a minefield to get there: low resources, high expectations and forests of doubt stood in between. But I believed it could be done. The challenge was to make others believe it, too, and equip them with everything they needed to succeed. But to find out what they needed from me, I first had to explain where we were headed. It's like taking a trip: what you pack depends on your destination. If you're setting sail for Aruba or Alaska, the contents of your suitcase will be wildly different.

Any time a leader steps up to share her vision, she also needs to be ready to invite debate, to ask questions and gather input and alternative views and take it all into consideration. There's no shortage of studies that find women excel at this aspect of leadership: communicating and doing it in a way that helps to build teams and relationships. Communicating goals, for instance, is about much more than simply telling folks what the results have to look like. It's a chance to motivate and inspire people by framing objectives in terms of opportunities, as in, *"Here's what we're after, here's where we need to end up and I think we have it in us—how can you help get us there?"* Building and then articulating a vision is the first natural step in collaborating. Today, when no leader can succeed, let alone survive, as a lone wolf, collaboration is the key to the future. It's also another trait of a woman's leadership style. In 2014, the Ketchum Leadership Communication Monitor released a global study based on polling 6,509 people in 13 countries across 5 continents that found that a more "feminine" communication model is "one of the defining facets" of the new leadership era. The survey revealed that women not only scored better than men when it came to communicating in an open and transparent way (62 percent vs. 38 percent), but also in the ability to bring out the best in others (61 percent vs. 39 percent). I was counting on my ability to do that as I made plans to explain CBC's new programming vision to staff and outside producers across the country.

Just eight weeks into the job, I hit the road on a multi-city tour to tell producers that the CBC had hours to fill and that each one of them was an opportunity. I brought my programming team, who were new to me but known to many in the audiences. I spoke to huge groups of people in hotel banquet halls and convention centres, letting them know exactly what CBC-TV wanted and what we didn't—series over movies of the week, and dramas, comedies and reality stories with casts that reflected the many cultures and colours of the Canadians watching—people who looked and sounded like them, their friends, their neighbours. I opened the doors wide to new program pitches. I streamlined the sluggish approvals process to make sure selected shows moved quickly into development. I reviewed scripts, revamped schedules and overhauled plans for packaging and promotion to give our new picks the best pop off the top. It was a hell of a pace. But I knew I wasn't just up against the clock. Suspicion and skepticism greeted my every move.

I had, after all, been brought into the public broadcaster by Richard Stursberg, the executive vice-president whose bids to make the CBC popular and profitable had also made him some enemies. Stursberg had headhunted me at Alliance Atlantis, where I had remodelled the content of its specialty channels, including the Food Network and HGTV, with hit shows that made household names of Mike Holmes, Sarah Richardson and the Designer Guys. This had typecast me as "Richard's gal from lifestyle TV"—i.e., the queen of froth. Before my stint at Alliance, I'd run programming at the multiple international broadcast channels of Hallmark Entertainment based in the United States, overseeing a $300 million budget and staff located worldwide. At Paragon, I'd been on the other side of the table, selling to international broadcasters, including the BBC and the CBC too. But my track record hardly registered with some CBC veterans who doubted I knew anything about running serious television. My unconventional profile puzzled them, perhaps even scared them. I was an outsider, so outside that no one had seen me coming. In many ways, that first upfront was really *my* coming out.

Traditionally, fall marks the start of a new television season. As summers fade and school starts, networks have touted fall launches for their new shows for almost as long as televisions have flickered in North American living rooms. But I opted to break with tradition, and put my money on the dead of winter. Before cable, PVRs and the Internet upended standard notions of programming schedules, I bet that a January launch for many of the shows would give the CBC's new lineup the chance it needed to shine outside the shadow of September's big American debuts. Inside the CBC, people rolled their eyes, believing this decision was yet further evidence that I was out of my depth. But my instinct told me that launching in a dead-of-winter lull that leans toward post-holiday hibernation in front of TV sets was worth the gamble.

So there I was onstage at that upfront, ready to unveil my first CBC-TV schedule. Knowing I was injecting enough surprise in the schedule itself, I stuck to the CBC's dry-as-toast format of years past in presenting it (*on Mondays at eight, we'll have this . . . at eight-thirty, we'll have that . . .*). The highlight, I hoped, was the content. We introduced *Dragon's Den*, where entrepreneurs pitch venture capitalists for investment, *Intelligence, Little Mosque on the Prairie* and *The Hour* with George Stroumboulopoulos, many of which would become big hits. I discussed the strategy behind the new programming and timing, and the plans to revitalize the CBC. And I told the crowd, "The stakes are high, the need is urgent, but the rewards will be great."

Yet in the media coverage that followed, what I'd said seemed to grab only slightly more attention than how I looked. Media reports described me as the "whip-thin" blonde in a dress and high-heel shoes. They noted my relative youthfulness and long hair. One blogger actually dubbed me the "kittenish programming mistress." When I eagerly checked to see the press reaction to the new lineup, I realized that my appearance had somehow become the frame of the story. I was mortified.

Women are invariably scrutinized, and criticized, for their appearance. The higher they climb the more subjected they become to the dated biases of others. Christine Lagarde, head of the International Monetary Fund, has been singled out as a fashion icon but also skewered for being "too elegant." For a time, Hillary Clinton's pantsuits had their own paparazzi. This kind of attention, sadly, speaks to the relative novelty of having a woman at the helm—and to the archaic pundits, and now the Internet hordes, still drawing lines around how women should look. More than three thousand years after Egypt's first female pharaoh sat bare-chested on her throne in a man's kilt and a full metal beard, women still wear the pressure to conform like a heavy cloak. After that first upfront, I donned mine.

Comments on my looks have always struck me as a kind of litmus test for attitudes toward women in leadership. By old standards, I embody the unexpected, and did at the CBC in particular. Unlike the older men who had come before me, I was in my thirties, and yes, blonde. In my first week on the job, I was mistaken for my own assistant (*"Can you give this memo to Kirstine when you see her?"*) Being underestimated can have its benefits as well as its drawbacks. While the scrutiny tends to make women particularly hyperaware of their looks, the truth is that at some point all leaders, male and female, make very conscious choices about what their appearance projects. Mark Zuckerberg's hoodie is as deliberate as the demure cardigan couture of Yahoo CEO Marissa Mayer.

What nagged at me was the suggestion that a nice dress and high heels projects an image that says "This woman lacks substance." By the media's measure, my appearance painted me as someone who spent more time shopping than working. It signalled "trivial and frivolous." Influenced by old models of feminism, it's an attitude too often perpetuated by women themselves: to be taken seriously, a female must eschew make-up, choose sensible shoes over pumps, resist any garment or accessory that might raise an unplucked eyebrow about her ability to do a job. Otherwise, she could set back generations of feminist activism. And, initially, that's how I reacted to the media spin.

At the time, I wasn't angry at what was said about how I looked, I was mortified. I felt that I had insulted the place I was trying to represent, drawing attention away from the network's transformation to shiny, blonde me. My inner critic was off and running . . . imagining the men, asking, "Who's that chick on the stage?" And the women thinking "silly girl" or worse—that I was actually trying to court attention. I thought the buzz should have been focused squarely on the content, the controversy of bringing reality TV to the CBC, or launching an unlikely sitcom about Muslims in a post 9/11 world. But the "lifestyle-TV gal" leading the charge seemingly looked too glamorous to be taken seriously. I decided I needed to tone myself down, cut my hair and buy flats. If I wanted to be taken seriously, I had to dress, or dress down, to suit the role.

Then something remarkable happened. In the weeks after I had appeared on that stage, people in the building started to figure out who I was as I walked the halls. No one mistook me for my assistant anymore. One day, about a week after the upfront, a young woman stopped me to say, "It's so great you're here. We don't see a lot of bosses like you . . . It's so great to see a woman doing the job!"

It dawned on me that I'd gone from suspect new kid on the block to something of a role model to these young women. Despite my own misgivings, my unconventional looks had distinguished me as a new *kind* of leader, especially among that emerging generation of women. They saw in me a person they could be. I suddenly realized how easy it can be to cower to criticism and to the idea that you should step back in line. But these women, my co-workers, some younger and others older, made a point to encourage me ("You go, Kirstine!" "Such a breath of fresh air!"). Their support took me completely by surprise and reminded me that the vocal opinion of a stodgy few was meaningless when others—without soapbox or agenda— found the prospect of a new way to lead so hopeful, exciting and maybe even inspiring. Exactly what message would I send by allowing pointed comments in media coverage to rob me of the freedom to be who I want to be? If I second-guessed the way I looked and dressed, and had always dressed—right back to my cash-strapped earliest days at Paragon when I bought the fabrics and Vogue patterns to sew my own clothes—that insecurity would eventually undermine me. Why would I give more weight to the negative comments than those that were supportive? It's a lesson I have to keep relearning, but in a world where those negative voices can be amplified by the very platforms I now work with, it's a big part of the strength that keeps me moving forward. Use the positive support around you to build the resilience you need to deal with the negative.

Owning Yourself

IF THE FIRST TASK OF LEADING is to figure out your goals, the first responsibility has to be the capacity to lead yourself—to understand and stand up for your values, your vision, and yes, your own style. To be anything other than authentic will inevitably compromise your confidence. It will also compromise the trust others place in you. You can't lead effectively, or for long, without earning and keeping the trust of people you work with. Authenticity matters, and it matters more today than it ever did. When the line between public and private has blurred, when so many interactions take place in a virtual sphere, a leader has to walk her talk. No one should be defined by the expectations of others, especially not by those who feel it's their business to dictate what success looks like.

When I was at the public broadcaster, sometimes there were suggestions—whispers, blogs, innuendo—that my success had to involve sex, one way or another. I even ended up on the cover of *Frank* magazine with talk-show host George Stroumboulopoulos amid allegations we were dating—we weren't! But the gossip magazine, along with more than a few souls at the CBC, assumed there had to be something going on. George had had a show on CBC's Newsworld when I arrived, and after I'd watched it, I thought here's this great young interviewer who could bring to the network a quirky late-night chat show that featured Canadians. At the time, there was no other late-night show that did that. But people assumed that we had to be fooling around or why else would I promote this dude with an earring who used to be on MuchMusic. Which is how the rumours, and our pictures, landed in *Frank*, and then became fodder for a rather rape-y fictional sex scene in my office that an odious blogger dreamed up.

It was a campaign, the first of a few I've seen, this one designed to keep me in my place and send a message to George that he hadn't earned his success. Landing multiple awards and critical kudos—as well as a place on US television and now as the host of the most popular show on Canadian TV, *Hockey Night in Canada*—was one way George responded. I didn't shrink from supporting George's ongoing growth with the network, but ignoring the whispers wasn't easy. Though it helped a lot when other women, many of them producers in TV and radio, told me they had also experienced the same kind of rumour campaign on the shows they had helmed.

But my daughters didn't have the benefit of that perspective. Suddenly, I had to tell my girls not to look at things in the paper, not to believe things they happened to see, or hear, and that if they had any questions they should ask me about them. My oldest daughter, who was eleven, took to policing the web on my behalf, "reporting abuse" whenever she spotted nasty comments online. But by the time all of this unfolded, I had already had my inner reckoning. And I was determined not to change a thing about the way I looked, dressed or acted to please or to counter the petty and salacious judgements of a few.

Unfortunately, women have been boxed in by social stereotypes for so long (virgins, vamps, mother hens, gossips, dumb blondes, shrews, bitches and on and on it goes) that we pay a high price fighting our way out. We can be so fearful of falling into one of these categories that we become afraid to be ourselves, afraid of not being liked or accepted, not taken seriously, of ruffling feathers. In the end, it's tempting to throw all kinds of walls up around our true selves. On a flight recently, I read an article in *Porter* magazine that once again explored the idea that self-doubt among high-achieving women—a.k.a.,

Imposter Syndrome—has become a chronic condition of the twenty-first century. What stuck with me were the words of a fifty-five-year-old CEO of a very successful PR firm who said of her professional self, "I put her on when I go to work." She viewed the successful professional that she presented to the world as a fake, and was finding it harder and harder to "put her on." Her closet told the story: she chose clothes to suit the tastes of the people she was meeting that day, cladding herself in hippie suede to meet the creative types, florals for clients, black suits for business. She had dressed to please others for so long she had forgotten what pleased *her*, which left her angry, feeling isolated and exhausted. I didn't doubt it. But I take heart in the fact that, increasingly, women are talking openly about the pressures, both internal and external, that they face when they attempt to fit like square pegs into limiting, imaginary holes. The only hope of overcoming these kinds of pressures is to drown them out with smarter voices— our own included. The spontaneous words of women I didn't even know reminded me of that in those early days at the CBC; with the reach of social media, women's voices are carrying far and wide.

At Twitter, the movement to stop defining women by how they look or what they wear is one of the more popular conversations on the platform. #AskHerMore, for instance, encourages red-carpet reporters at the Oscars and other awards ceremonies to ask female celebrities about more than their frocks and accessories. The hashtag was launched in 2014 by the Representation Project, a California-based group that aims to eradicate harmful stereotypes, especially those that hold women back, and it's not just celebrities who champion the cause. As one woman tweeted last March: "Bradley Cooper gets asked about the community of actors and Lupita [Nyong'o] gets asked about her dress." As Reese Witherspoon said, "We're more than just our dresses."

The point is that not only should we not allow outdated ideas to box us in, we should go further and take pride in the traits that distinguish us as individuals, the characteristics, whatever they may be, that make each of us different. To be sure, it's still a man's world, and a white man's world at that, but if today's chiefs and rulers are any barometer, the winds of change are blowing everywhere. All around us is evidence that leaders can be who they want to be, project whatever image they want to project and be recognized for what they achieve, not judged or held back by their gender, youth or high heels, the colour of their skin or the sex of their partner. The rules are being rewritten, and in many cases, erased. We're living in a time when the premier of Canada's most populous province is openly lesbian, where a black man is the president of the United States, where the founder of Facebook can lead one of the world's largest companies in a hoodie; and a woman can run the CBC in heels—high and red.

The highest-paid female chief executive in the US is a beautiful case in point: She started life as a man. Martine Rothblatt, who earned $38 million in 2013, and made a previous fortune as a founder of Sirius radio, went on to launch United Therapeutics, the Maryland-based pharmaceutical company she now runs. A recent *New York* magazine profile of Rothblatt quoted a friend of Martine's who said the subject of her gender never came up: "Bright people don't talk about these things. The body is but a shell. It's the mind and the heart that count."

Hiding who you are is not a value in the information age. And, like it or not, despite all the ways you think you can be anonymous on the Internet, hiding is increasingly harder to pull off when social media makes it possible to share parts of our lives, and the lives of others, in intimate ways: family photos, movies we watch, celebratory milestones, wins, losses, likes, dislikes and ordinary moments. The more we share the more we invite others to connect, and connections are key to building networks in the personal and professional spheres of our lives; networks, as we all know, are the breeding grounds of opportunity. The ability to be yourself, and show the world all the ways you are who you are, has become something to trade on. It might make you uncomfortable or wistful for walls, but in the web-driven selfie world, there is a perceived value in a certain vanity; it's not a character flaw, it's a commodity.

Mommy bloggers have made small fortunes reviewing products that feature in their families' lives. Job interviews are becoming desk-top auditions. (Jennifer Lawrence actually landed her Oscar-winning role in *Silver Linings Playbook* with a Skype audition from her parents' home in Kentucky.) Instagram, YouTube and Snapchat create celebrities bigger than movie stars, and not just the Justin Bieber variety. Consider Michelle Phan, a struggling young student and waitress in Florida, who uploaded how-to makeup videos, attracted more than a million views, got a $1 million contract from Google to create more; four million clicks later, she found herself sponsored by L'Oréal with her own line of cosmetics.

Standing out amid the world's noise and clutter, online and off, can be an advantage, a competitive edge. And after a few bruising weeks, that's how I came to see my own story at the CBC. Fighting dated perceptions that success had to look a certain way, or that smart and serious had to mean bland, was a key battle in the war to modernize the network. At HGTV and the Food Network, I'd seen how we could create domestic "stars" in Canada, but it did mean bucking convention and then taking on that all-too-Canadian urge to clip its tall poppies. To succeed I had to cultivate a bit of a red-carpet sensibility at the public broadcaster, to recast it as a place where hits were made, stardom was possible and women could still be "more than just our dresses."

Next, Buy into Your People

A COUPLE OF YEARS INTO MY TIME at Alliance Atlantis, I organized a field trip. The executives from HGTV and the Food Network were, as you might imagine, passionate about helping people live their best lives and were expert in the ways of duck confit, Le Creuset cookware and elegant decor. Increasingly, the program pitches that caught their discerning eye reflected the best in taste and style, shows that would elevate the experience and expertise of the audience. They were aimed at people who had all the right knives and all the right pans and all the right tastes. The lives they presented were exquisite, the locales even more so. I asked, "But what about the people watching in Moncton who only have time to shop for their potatoes and their pillows at Walmart? How do they relate to *Fine Cooking* and *World of Interiors* when they're reading *Canadian Living*?" We had focused so hard on presenting the best, most exotic and aspirational shows that we were at risk of building a dreamland that depressed rather than inspired.

Without a real research budget to prove my instincts about our target audience, I decided to take the networks' executives on a train ride out of Toronto and as far west into suburbia as a GO ticket could carry us. I had a real estate agent meet us at the other end and show us around four houses for sale—two-storey family homes and townhouses—and I told the executives to take a good look inside each one. They were homes decorated with care, down to the accent cushions bought at the local big-box store. The restaurants in the neighbourhood served good solid family fare, and, on a big celebration night, people went to Milestones, not the local bistro. We glimpsed the world of people living their best lives while shopping at Costco and ripping recipes out of magazines they picked up in the supermarket checkout line. And my reasons for giving us all a peek into those lives were straightforward: We had to get out of our little urban bubble. We had to recognize that people, their choices and their aspirations, were different everywhere, and those differences mattered.

It turned out to be a trip worth taking. Not only did we bond as a team, the shows they pitched after that fact-finding mission had a whole different feel. We went from gourmet fare and unpronounceable ingredients to shows such as *Licence to Grill,* from *Dream Castles* to *Property Virgins,* programs that invited everyone to explore exciting but accessible possibilities on the home front. Sure, it was still worth seeking to inspire and elevate viewers, but if you make them feel like they don't belong in the tent, they'll never enter it, and you'll never reach them at all.

The experience of that field trip to the suburbs came back to me in those early months at the CBC. In many ways, it looked like the public broadcaster was losing touch with the people it was serving, and the distance was costing them dearly by every measure that mattered. CBC's staffers were committed to producing high-quality, critically acclaimed programming, but making shows that would also reach the wide audience of taxpayers who supported the broadcaster seemed less their focus. They had also lost faith in their own abilities to create hits. Of course I couldn't put the staff of the CBC on a train anywhere to help connect them with viewers, but I could go to them to talk about why we *had to* think beyond the white walls of our headquarters on Front Street. It would also give me the chance to hear from them directly how they felt about the network, what mattered to them, and whether, together, we could reach that common ground.

If the first step in leading is to know yourself, discovering what matters to those around you lands right behind. You have to understand a corporate culture before you can hope to change it. And in these times, when technology is forcing all enterprise to adapt to the rapidly changing market, that's a principle with broad applications.

I knew it wouldn't be easy. Of all the challenges I faced when I arrived at the CBC, getting the team to embrace a new culture of possibilities was the most daunting, as it tends to be in any organization. New leaders can be tempted to simply clean house, sweep out the personnel of past regimes and surround themselves with a new guard. I could tell I had surprised a lot of them by not firing them all and starting from scratch. But coming into a workplace as storied, and complicated, as the CBC, I knew I needed the help of people with a history at the organization who understood how things work, and what didn't work. I had to depend on their experience to even get a footing in the place. Digging deep to find out what people know, what they value and what their goals actually are is key to having influence—and influence, not control, is the new power, a concept I'll tackle in a later chapter. It comes down to emotional intelligence. Exercising that kind of smarts was never thought to be a necessity in the corner office, but today it's indispensable. I don't think you can ever truly change someone's internal value structure. But by learning what they value most and what they want to achieve, you can work out where their ideas intersect with and support your overall vision. You can't get buy-in from people until you have bought into them.

I could prize promptness above all, and expect everyone to show up to every meeting on time and prepared to work. You could think meetings are the worst waste of time because being out in the field getting the job done is your top priority. But we are not that far apart in our shared values. You and I both value dedication to the job, we just approach it differently. If you can demonstrate how those values fit within the broader framework for the success you envision—show that you really are shooting for the same net—suddenly you find you're on the same side, building a team that you can lead in new directions.

Research has found that women tend to be particularly good at finding common ground, asking the right questions, the right way, and actively listening for points of potential connection. In a 2011 survey, the *Harvard Business Review* examined how these "nurturing" competencies of leadership vary between women and men. Using data from 7,280 international leaders in corporate, government and organizational spheres, private and public, it found that women significantly outscored men in their ability to inspire and motivate others, communicate powerfully, collaborate, build relationships and establish long-term goals. The idea that female leaders are naturally nurturing, sensitive and compassionate might sound like a motherhood issue, but the research discovered that women also excel in areas of taking initiative and driving results, characteristics long thought to be strengths associated with male leaders. That the *Harvard Business Review*, a venerable bastion of management insight, took the time to analyze these soft-touch attributes, speaks to the larger point that they have become crucial traits of modern leaders, male or female. Increasingly, being a nice guy is simply good for business.

Whether being a woman shaped my efforts to bridge differences and build a unified team at the CBC, I can't say. I do know that it wasn't customary for the male leaders who came before me to leave the so-called "white fortress on Front Street" to travel across the country and ask the CBC's own people what they thought was up with this place and how they would define success for the CBC. I made it my business to speak to as many people as I could—one-on-one, over coffee, at town halls—from television, radio, news, advertising, marketing, all departments.

For many of the employees I talked with, "metrics" was the big worry. They feared that I'd be sitting in a corner office dictating how we'd get a million viewers an airing, and that any show that missed that mark would fall from the schedules. They were also sure that chasing ratings would mean I'd be about "dumbing down" the CBC, because in their interpretation, popular could only mean lowbrow, which fuelled fears that the public broadcaster was about to lose its identity as the country's hallowed purveyor of high-quality content.

They were important conversations to have, in part because they gave me a chance to explain my broader mandate. The one-million-viewer mark was a goal, sure, but really just one step in attaining the big prize, which to my mind was, and always had been, for the CBC to really mean something to more Canadians. During the three-month lockout of CBC employees the year before I started, a discouraging Decima poll taken in the midst of the bitter labour dispute had suggested only 10 percent of Canadians missed CBC programming enough to consider the loss of it a "major inconvenience." I wanted the network to be more vital than that. I felt Canadians deserved to have something they wanted to watch on their public broadcaster. Otherwise they'd be right to think of it as a waste of taxpayers' money. As I told a reporter in my first interview after accepting the CBC job, my definition of success would be standing on a street corner and hearing someone say, "Hey, did you see that great show on CBC last night?"

But the major hurdle was persuading people that "popular" was not a synonym for "dumb." Many worried that high ratings and high-quality programming were incompatible. When I asked how they defined "high quality," they often fell back on the "I know it when I see it" argument. Yet what I saw, and what I tried to persuade many of them to see, was a tragic disconnect that prioritizes winning New York Festivals awards over producing programming that Canadians connect with—dangerous, especially, when it's the viewers who pay for the CBC.

Producing programs both smart and popular, I thought, was the best way out of the hole we'd fallen into. If we didn't make shows people wanted to watch, we risked losing even more relevancy—and revenue: the advertisers would turn away. At the time, government funding covered about half of what it took to run the CBC. If there was a drop in advertising revenue, we'd be in big trouble. It was a very fine balancing act for sure, but I was certain we could get there. And once we'd earned trust from both the audience and advertisers, we could take them to really interesting and adventurous places. But that would take time. We had to lay the groundwork and build.

For every *Murdoch Mysteries*—one of the most popular and acclaimed series on the network—programmers created the breathing room to try something more risky elsewhere on the schedule, as we did in 2008 with *The Kids in the Hall: Death Comes to Town*. It was a delicate balance but one we needed in order to survive, to pay the bills for essentials such as television news, which, done right, was expensive, and radio, which was less so, but didn't generate revenue. CBC had a lot of important reasons not just to exist but to thrive, and it was putting itself in jeopardy by not grabbing the reins where it could.

Not everyone agreed with me. When I toured the country talking to staffers, I also held town halls, along with the heads of comedy and drama, to ask viewers what they wanted to see on their public broadcaster. I brought my schedule of the new programs I'd lined up, and some in the audience were livid, particularly diehard CBC fans with a long-standing connection to the network. One evening on the east coast, a famous local actor stood up and said, "How dare you! You're a public broadcaster and you're doing reality TV?"

"Okay," I said, "is there a public broadcaster you think that we should look up to? Who should we be emulating?"

"The BBC," he replied.

I reminded him that the BBC broadcast *Who Wants To Be a Millionaire?*, *Dancing with the Stars* and *Who Do You Think You Are?*—all reality-TV programs. And, unlike the CBC, the BBC had chosen to run these popular shows without any need to generate ad revenue. (The BBC is funded by the sale of television licences, and has no need to supplement its government funding with commercials in order to survive.)

That heated exchange was emblematic of the unrealistic expectations thrown at the CBC. But step by step, we renovated the creaky primetime schedule, adding popular shows like *Being Erica*, reinvesting in stalwarts like *The Nature of Things* and *The National*, and *Wheel of Fortune* (yes, we aired that show, too!) started to turn in CBC-TV's favour.

Then Deliver the Goods

THERE ARE MOMENTS AS A LEADER when speed and decisiveness matter above all else. Being decisive endures as one of the critical attributes of any leader, especially when these days of big data present opportunities, and dilemmas, by the gigabyte. Decision-making has generally been synonymous with taking action, which may be why it's traditionally considered a strength of male leaders, as in a "man of action." Presumably, in the evolutionary scheme of things, bringing home the bison demanded instant decisions about fight or flight. For women, who excel at gathering knowledge, encouraging input and weighing options, speed is thought to be less of a strong suit, and there's a cart of psychological baggage that comes with that concept. Making quick decisions increases the risk of making the wrong decision, and fear of risk and failure is notorious for keeping women in the workplace tethered to the status quo (another point I'll be exploring later).

But there's also another dynamic at work, and it's one of the more insidious forms of gender stereotyping in the workplace, whether you call it "the double-bind," implicit bias or, as it was dubbed in a 2014 Catalyst paper, "damned or doomed." All these terms describe the idea that a female leader compelled to make fast decisions can be caught in a no-win situation. If she doesn't act fast, she is seen as too soft to lead; if she does, she's viewed as unlikeable. Or, as Sylvia Ann Hewlett, co-director of the Women's Leadership Program at Columbia Business School, describes it in her recent book, *Executive Presence,* women are regarded as in-effective if they "can't make up their minds" and as cold-hearted bitches when they do. Women, Hewlett argues, should at least "appear to be decisive." That suggests it's better to make the wrong decision than no decision at all—in other words, go brave or go home. Speed is the key.

I don't disagree. But in my view, this is where the digital age can serve women well. Now more than ever, agility and decisiveness have to be core strengths of leadership, and when women have so many characteristics essential for lead-ing successful teams, we have to trust *the way* in which women tend to make decisions. We are inclined to be infor-mation gatherers, to seek input and do our homework.

There's fascinating research, for instance, including a 2012 report from Barclays Wealth and Ledbury Research, that finds women are less likely than men to buy shares in companies they know little about, regardless of whether analysts dub it a "hot stock." And that cautious research-before-investing approach results in women trading less often than men—and losing less than men. The Barclays study found that women investors are more likely than men to make money in the market; a seminal 2001 report from behavioural economists at the University of California found women's returns outpaced those of men by an average of 1.4 percent annually. Gathering information and input—a ton of it—in order to make informed decisions fast has never been simpler. Knowledge of all kinds is a click away, whether it's you or the team that's mining it.

Some may consider this research-style approach cautious, or even overly cautious. Others would say it's smart. And today technology gives us the tools to gather information deeper and faster than ever before. So those informed decisions can come quicker than ever before. A 2013 study from researchers at McMaster University's DeGroote School of Business surveyed six hundred board directors and found that *how* women make decisions makes them better corporate leaders. Companies with women on their boards are well known to outperform those who don't have female members, and the DeGroote paper found that women's collaborative, information-intensive approach is more likely to result in sound decisions—even if they are those that rock the boat. So when it comes to swift decisions, women need to be courageous, take a moment to draw upon all that they've learned, heard and seen, and then move forward.

After the months I'd spent in conversation with people at the CBC, for example, what I had to do next was show them we could deliver. Nothing does more to galvanize a team than positive results. Which is why I couldn't afford to wait until my second season on the job to demonstrate that success was possible. The network needed an almost instant hit to quiet the naysayers and lift the gloom. They had to see that we had the goods to create a smart hit—and all I had to do was my job, which was to exercise my influence to make that happen, starting with spreading the word.

In the not too distant past, one of the tried-and-true ways to let people know about a new program was to promote it during peak hours, and preferably during a show with a massive audience. At the time, the only show that captured a million viewers on a weekly basis was *Hockey Night in Canada,* an American hockey blogger once dubbed this country's crack cocaine. That made it a powerful vehicle to draw attention to other shows and everybody at the network vied for its promo spots—including me, the boss. I saw it as the perfect launching pad for *Little Mosque on the Prairie,* but reaction from our sports department was less than warm. They weren't in favour of donating valuable airtime to promo a show that they thought would never attract the same kind of audience that tuned in to hockey on a Saturday night. Hockey dudes aren't going to watch a show like *Little Mosque,* they told me. But hockey wasn't just for the guys, I said, it was for families—families watch hockey and they'll watch *Little Mosque.* Sure, it was a risk, but as I told the sports department, sparing the new show a couple of promos wouldn't kill them.

The *Little Mosque* premiere was scheduled for a Tuesday night in January, and we pulled out all the stops to stoke interest in advance with an extensive promo campaign. This included handing out Christmas cookies at malls, gingerbread women dressed in hijabs. It was, after all, a comedy. (I did turn down the marketing pitch to fly an ultralight plane around the CN Tower trailing a promo written in Arabic: um, what were they thinking?) The show would follow the *Rick Mercer Report*, which claimed a weekly audience share of close to a million. I asked if Rick, the biggest star on CBC's primetime schedule, would do a personal throw to the show during his sign-off that night, and he agreed. *The National* also aired a piece, "Will *LMOP* save the CBC?" The little show with the strange title also brought CNN, Fox News and a whack of other media calling to hear more. On the day it debuted, the BBC carried an online story on *Little Mosque* that became the most downloaded article on its website. No pressure . . .

The day after *Little Mosque*'s first episode aired, I was sitting in a boardroom with a bunch of finance types reviewing budgets when the person in charge of scheduling sent me a message. The daily ratings report card had just come in and her one line of text read "218 OMG." I was bewildered. After all that effort, only 218,000 people had watched? But then I looked at the message again. Was it actually saying 218,000 or did it mean 2.2 million? I pushed back from the table, opened the boardroom door and down the hall I heard screaming. Of the most glorious kind. They were *celebrating*. It *was* 2.2 million. We'd never seen any number like that, and the record stands today.

People were beyond happy. They felt exhilarated and exonerated. We had a bona fide hit so big that, ironically, the guys from hockey called to ask me for a promo spot for *Hockey Night in Canada* on *Little Mosque* for the following week. (When it aired in its regular Wednesday time slot, the same premiere episode garnered another 1.7 million viewers.) I suggested we run a huge ad to announce that the show was, officially, "Canada's biggest hit." The staff was hesitant, unaccustomed to the idea of positive attention—and uncomfortable with vying for it. "Ooooh, we don't know if we should say that . . ." they told me. But I coaxed them to go along with it, to take a bow and be proud of their great work: it was theirs—ours—to enjoy.

The feeling of triumph buoyed the building, lifting the pressure of gloom and pessimism. I sent Peter Mansbridge a cheeky note asking whether *The National* wanted to do a follow-up to "Will *LMOP* save the CBC?" I felt joy, not simply because of the success, but because people had seen that their success was possible. To me, it was a victory that took us much closer to the goal we were aiming for. Who doesn't feel better about themselves and their organization, more confident, more ambitious, when they know their team can hit it out of the park?

As it turned out, that January signalled the start of a veritable hit parade for the CBC. It's not that all ratings wowed as soon as the shows were launched, as *Little Mosque*'s did. But many shows that debuted on CBC-TV in my early years went on to earn loyal followings, such as *The Hour* and *Dragon's Den* (now in its tenth season, having turned the word "dragon" into a national synonym for venture capitalist), *Republic of Doyle* and *Heartland*, which in 2015 became the longest-running one-hour scripted drama in the history of Canadian television.

I wasn't any genius: change had to happen at the CBC one way or another. The people I led had everything to do with fulfilling what I saw as the urgent need to connect with Canadian viewers. The field trip to the suburbs had evolved. We developed direct and effective methods to tap into the desires of audiences. During the 2012–13 NHL lockout, for example, we relied on an online poll of audiences to find out what famous hockey matchups they'd like to see replayed and their answers determined which games we broadcast. We also made it a point to reach out to new Canadians through focus groups, surveys and interviews, which resulted in us making the move to broadcast *Hockey Night in Canada* in Punjabi. These were initiatives that not only spoke to new successes, and new ways to explore what viewers wanted, but also continued to stoke the spirits of people within the CBC, proving to them that change was possible. I'd drawn on my experience to make that happen, but it also took a certain courage and confidence to ignore the boundaries that others had set. That courage and confidence, I believe, is something that all leaders, but women in particular, have to be able to tap if they are going to succeed.

When I took the stage in 2007 to offer a look at our lineup for the following season, I threw out the old presentation format. The CBC's ratings were the highest they'd been in five years and we had nine new homegrown shows to unveil. Instead of plodding methodically through the primetime schedule hour by hour, we created our own live variety show, with music, comedy, video clips from the programs to come, live interviews with cast members and a host of CBC talent. We impressed the ad buyers. Our shows wowed our guests. In that moment, it was a celebration of our hard-won success as a team, however fleeting that turned out to be.

III

What Can Happen if You Don't Follow Your Dream

MY FATHER WAS BORN in a town in central Scotland. It was a small place, famous for a boarding school where generations of wealthy English families had sent their sons to be educated, but not just the wealthy made the cut. A bequest had endowed a scholarship so that the town's brightest boy could attend the school regardless of his family income. In the late 1940s, my father was that boy. His smarts earned him entry to the academy, where, it so happened, his mother, my grandmother, was also the school cleaner. I've often imagined how my dad felt in those class-obsessed days of his adolescence, trying to fit in with the upper-crust lads while his mother cleaned up after them.

At a time when all graduates went into service, my father joined the army. At a military base in England, he met my mother at a dance. They married at nineteen and twenty-one and within a year they were on a ship to Canada, hungry to carve out a better life. My father took a clerking job at a mining company and worked his way up to become head of its exploration division in Latin America.

My mother worked full-time as a draftsperson until she had children. But even after my sister and I were born, she found ways to turn her natural talent as an artist into extra income. Art was in her blood. Her father was a gifted painter who produced a notable portrait of Lord Robert Baden-Powell, the British baron who founded the Boy Scouts Association (my granddad was one of the original six Boy Scouts). Yet neither my grandfather, a scientist by profession, nor my mother, would have regarded art as a way to make a living. My mother used her artistic talents to make pocket money at craft shows, setting up a booth where she sold beautiful hand-knit sweaters that featured impressionist landscapes rendered in angora, silk and cashmere. In the corner of her booth, I knit, too, well enough that I eventually knit for people on commission, making sweaters and baby clothes.

I was always drawn to the arts—design, literature and music. All through school I played the flute, saxophone, oboe and clarinet. At the University of Toronto, I earned a coveted spot in the creative writing class of Josef Skvorecky. But I wanted to marry my talents with something concrete—a "real" job. I mixed courses in finance and other subjects in with my English lit classes. It's been a mantra of the Baby Boomers and the generations who followed that you should follow your dreams. But in my family, as with many immigrant households, making a good living was the dream that mattered most.

So I decided to go into publishing. Apart from my love of reading, I had no burning desire to actually be a publisher, but I thought the options of an English lit grad were limited, and teaching was not for me. In publishing I could earn a salary in a job that was at least related to creative writing. But when fate threw me into the television industry, I discovered that I could learn to love the job I'd stumbled into.

Down with the Five-Year Plan

THAT OPENNESS TO NEW OPPORTUNITIES, however unpredictable or unexpected, has been a major element of my success. When people, usually women, ask about my professional achievements, I can honestly say they have had more to do with taking chances than setting a career goal. I never set out to navigate a route to the top tier of any organization or corporation. To me, the most exciting career paths are those that unfold in unexpected ways. I am anti five-year-plan because in my experience the best things do not flow from making a plan and sticking to it. The key is to believe that you have what it takes not only to meet the challenges you find along the way, but to be open to what you learn on that journey. If you lock yourself into a single dream job you're desperate to attain, you may close yourself off from something even grander.

There's a growing recognition that following one's dreams or passions is no guarantee of success or happiness. Author Cal Newport, a computer scientist at Georgetown University, calls it the "passion trap" and suggests that passion may in fact be the root of widespread workplace unhappiness. In his recent book, *So Good They Can't Ignore You*, Newport argues that if people only seek out work they love, they are bound to become disillusioned when they fail to love the work they do and essentially find their dreams unfulfilled. The passion trap prevents people from pursuing opportunities that don't match their preconceived dreams.

As technology rapidly reshapes the global economy, relying on your dreams to guide your worklife could hold you back from what can make you truly happy. Traditional industries are being transformed (or failing) and traditional jobs are morphing and vanishing too. Today's list of dream jobs simply doesn't include the many possibilities for work that tomorrow is bound to bring. The US Department of Education, for instance, estimates that 60 percent of all new jobs created over the next two decades will require skills that only 20 percent of the current workforce possesses. The smart approach may be to unhook your ambitions from a particular plan because those plans are informed by the world of today where, according to the US Bureau of Labor Statistics, the demand for many traditional vocations is rapidly shrinking. For example, metal and plastic machine workers are increasingly not needed as manufacturing becomes more automated; so, too, mainstream journalists, whose numbers are diminishing along with traditional print outlets; travel agents who find it hard to compete with DIY travel sites; postal workers, as people write fewer letters; and so on. At the same time, new occupations are emerging in the knowledge economy that no one ever dreamed of at those old-school career fairs, jobs like directors of community engagement, brand strategists, chief experience officers. What's hopeful about this from a gender perspective is that none of these titles have a traditional gender. Say "doctor," "lawyer," or "taxman" and people still tend to picture, well, a man. But if you think "industrial-organizational psychologist," "genetic counsellor," or "information security analyst"—all occupations the Bureau of Labor Statistics predicts will grow robustly over the next decade—likely no gender comes to mind. Which is why today, for women, and men, too, keeping your mind open to the widest range of opportunities will reduce the chances you'll find yourself boxed in.

In my own case, when I arrived at Paragon Entertainment all those years ago, my unfamiliarity with the television industry was an asset. It prompted me to learn as much as I could. And as receptionist/girl Friday I got to see and hear it all. I was a blank slate, with the desire and curiosity not only to learn the business, but also to bring to it fresh ideas precisely because I was new. And in Isme Bennie, I found the perfect boss for an eager protegée, one who recognized my energy and encouraged my opinions. She threw me into challenges all on my own and also included me in on the high-level business deals she was negotiating. One thing we soon did together was look at shows that we might want to add to the roster we were selling to broadcasters worldwide, from Channel 9 Australia to HBO Ole.

One of the first shows I lobbied for reflected the kind of outside-the-box thinking a newbie can bring. Unlike the dramas and cartoon series that Paragon was known for, I thought the time was right to pick up a bare-bones how-to decorating show from a complete unknown. Her name was Debbie Travis, a former UK fashion model who had worked in TV editing and production. After moving to Montreal to be with her new husband, Hans Rosenstein, a video distributor who'd worked with Paragon, Debbie had time on her hands and she decided to paint and redecorate their old Victorian house. She did it with such style that clients came calling, so many that she and Hans produced an instructional video with Debbie demonstrating her crafty techniques in a show they called *The Painted House*.

I loved the idea instantly, and Isme agreed. Decorating shows like *Trading Spaces* and *Changing Rooms* had recently debuted in the UK and the US, and I had a strong sense that lifestyle-makeover programming was about to take off. Most home improvement programs until then had been of the *This Old House* variety, where someone with deep pockets took whole properties down to the studs and renovated them top to bottom. But *The Painted House* didn't feature historic mansions, just rooms—a makeover of a bathroom, a kitchen, a bedroom. All you need is "a little bit of paint" was Debbie's motto. It empowered people. She was self-taught and presented fantastically. With her model looks and Lancashire accent intact from her hometown in England's northwest, she sounded like she'd walked off the set of *Coronation Street*. As it turned out, *The Painted House* exceeded all expectations, in Canada and beyond. With infinite possibilities for time slots in the expanding cable universe, in primetime or daytime, it became a worldwide hit. It also proved to me that while I had no talent in front of the camera, I could spot it from behind.

You could call it a sixth sense or intuition. I think of it as an aptitude for stepping outside of myself, and the moment, to ask not whether *I* personally like something, but whether *others* will like it—metaphorically becoming part of the crowd and sensing what turns them on. I am not a fan of *Monster Trucks,* or an avid watcher of figure-skating specials, but I have represented both enthusiastically because I appreciate their appeal to others. I think this ability to have a bead on broad public tastes has always been with me. I love being able to spot "it"—that quality that makes someone or something shine above the rest. And I feel immense satisfaction when I get it right. Even as a kid, I used to listen to new releases from Madonna or early Duran Duran and be able to predict which song would be a hit. A few bars in, I could just tell. I dreamt about one day becoming a music industry executive, plucking potential stars out of the crowd. I dropped that dream in the midst of university applications and career-planning classes. But as fate would have it, I landed in a completely different career that allowed me to pick out the "it" and help make it shine.

The point is that if you're open to trying jobs you never imagined doing, you might discover strengths and talents you didn't know you had, or didn't recognize as professionally valuable. Sure, you may find out that you're not the right fit for a particular pursuit—but there's a lot to be said for learning what you don't like too. Either way, the common thread through all of this is confidence, believing that you have what it takes to capitalize on unexpected opportunities when they come along. But, as studies have repeatedly found, women are notoriously hard on themselves when it comes to recognizing their strengths and their ability to rise to a challenge.

In 2011, the Institute of Leadership and Management in the UK surveyed 3,000 male and female managers and found that women start out with lower ambitions for career advancement than their male counterparts. When it comes to applying for a promotion, 20 percent of men apply for a role despite only partially meeting its job description, compared to 14 percent of women. While 62 percent of men said they'd expected to be managers, only half of the women did. Men were more confident across all age groups (70 percent vs. 50 percent), and that confidence had a significant impact on the trajectory of their careers. With low confidence and lower expectations of reaching leadership and management roles, women, the study found, were less likely to achieve their ambitions. At the management level, the results were predictably similar: half of the women reported feeling self-doubt, while less than a third of male respondents expressed that.

It may be that males are less likely to tell a research team they have experienced self-doubt, or it may be that women are more self-aware and reflective and too often judge themselves and how they appear harshly—something I have struggled with myself. But regardless of what underlying forces might explain the gender difference in self-confidence levels, other research finds that success has as much to do with confidence as with competence. In part, because in the eyes of others, showing that you are self-assured goes a long way to reassuring them that you have what it takes to do the job.

Women aren't the only ones with work to do on this front. I'd say the far more insidious and stubborn barrier to women's advancement is still the entrenched belief that men are better suited to leading than women are. When McKinsey & Company investigated the factors that hold women back, it found that while companies have worked hard to eliminate overt discrimination, "women still face the pernicious force of mindsets that limit opportunity." Based on surveys of 2,500 men and women, interviews with 30 chief diversity officers and a review of 100 research papers, the 2011 report concluded that both male and female managers continue to remove viable female candidates from the running, often on the assumption that women can't handle certain jobs *and* take care of their families. At the same time, the study found that men are more often promoted on their potential, but women on their accomplishments. The upshot is that no matter how confident a woman may be, she has to do more than a man to prove she's worthy of advancement. This implicit bias is not easy to overcome, because it's hard to single out.

If there's good news to be drawn from the report it's the conclusion that companies now have every incentive to change those mindsets. When McKinsey researchers asked business executives to list the most important leadership attributes needed for success today, the top four—"intellectual stimulation, inspiration, participatory decision-making and setting expectations/rewards"—were traits more commonly found among women leaders.

The fact is that the very idea of what constitutes a leadership "strength" is expanding to encompass a wider and more eclectic range of qualities—and increasingly they're those generally considered to be feminine. Top business schools that have delved into this keep coming up with the same answers: the growing need for emotional intelligence in the corner office, social and interpersonal skills, the ability to actively listen, forge relationships, build teams, engender trust, drive consensus and communicate complex ideas simply. There are still enduring leadership traits considered more typically masculine, such as being focused, driven, decisive and assertive. But I think what's worth noting is that in the past neither men nor women have typically viewed "feminine" attributes as qualifying females for the corner office. Yet the greater appreciation women have for the diverse skills they bring to the table, the better able they are to help an organization succeed in these changing times, and themselves too.

Figuring Out When to Fold

KNOWING WHEN TO LEAVE A JOB can be as pivotal to career success as knowing when to take one. By the late nineties, that time had come for me at Paragon. Major changes were under way in the broadcast industry that would also change the distribution business. For years we'd been selling shows to a growing and hungry roster of international broadcasters. But as those networks matured, they saw increasing value in creating, not renting, the programs they aired. The days of selling a movie-of-the-week to multiple networks for millions of dollars were ending. This was most obvious to me on a trip to a broadcast festival in Cannes where I had two networks in Germany bidding fiercely for a TV movie starring *General Hospital* soap star Jack Wagner. The competition was driving up the price considerably, when, literally overnight, one of the networks withdrew its offer. When I asked why, I learned that my two vying networks had just merged. The bidding war was over. Consolidating would not only allow them to acquire that movie for less, it would give them a better shot at creating their own content.

The penny dropped hard for me. I didn't want to stay on the side of selling programming to networks. I wanted to build a network that made and commissioned its own programming. At the same time, the principals at Paragon were running into financial trouble over losing bets they'd made on feature films. They'd taken to drawing on the profits from the distribution division so that my division's bills were suddenly going unpaid. I didn't like the outlook for the future.

When a headhunter contacted me about becoming general manager and vice-president of programming at Trio/Newsworld International, a US cable channel that reached thirty million American homes, I didn't hesitate— even though it meant leaving behind my "president" title. Earlier that year, I'd given birth to my first child, and Paragon's CEO, concerned that my departure might say too much about the overall health of the company, told people I was leaving because I wanted to "take it easy" since becoming a mother. I made it my business to let him and my contacts know that slowing down had nothing to do with it. I was leaving for a better professional opportunity.

The content at Trio had been built to appeal to Canadian expats in the United States with a lineup of all-Canadian shows, like *Traders* and *The Littlest Hobo*. But its owners, the Desmarais family of Power Corporation, realized the independent channel could no longer stand alone in a sea of ever-greater consolidation among broadcasters. They intended to fix it up to sell it, revamping the network's programming to increase its popularity and profitability in order to make it more attractive to potential buyers. In other words, if I did my job well, eventually I wouldn't have one. Trio would be sold. But, to me, gaining the experience of reinventing and rebranding a network made the move worthwhile. (And Paragon went into receivership six months after I left.)

To boost its value, I figured Trio had to break away from running only Canadian shows, so I set a plan in motion to transform it by infusing it with international shows that would appeal to the viewer curious about the world around them. (This was before people could find everything from everywhere online.) Picking up movie packages and original dramas from around the world, such as *Cracker* with Robbie Coltrane from the UK and the *Rebus* detective series featuring Scotland's John Hannah, I grew the network's worth and profile within a year. Big players came calling, including Disney and NBC. By 2000, the transformation landed Power Corp a handsome sale of the channel to USA Networks for US$155 million. The Desmarais family was so happy with the deal that they gave everyone who had worked at the company a DVD player, an expensive gift at the time. They wanted to fly me from Toronto to their head office in Montreal for a dinner in order to present my gift to me in person. I was nearly eight months pregnant with my second child and I tried to decline. They wouldn't hear of it, and so I went, waddling, and after the dinner they took me aside and handed me an envelope. Inside was a cheque, for more money than I had ever seen in one lump. It wasn't part of my contract (I didn't have one) or my compensation, but a thank-you for a job well done. Their generosity touched me deeply and taught me a great deal about the importance of respecting the people who work for you, and showing how much you appreciate their contributions, just as I had learned from Isme Bennie the value of rewarding initiative.

Risky Business

THE JOB PROSPECTS FOR ME in Canada after leaving Trio were grim. Canadian cable networks had yet to take off and there was little demand for my particular brand of programming expertise. I had no choice but to cast a wide net. The new owners of Trio had mentioned the possibility of a broadcasting job in New York, but with a toddler and a newborn, and a husband who had just finished teachers' college, the idea of putting in long hours in Manhattan didn't make sense for us. But then a headhunter told me about a major job opportunity in Denver that sounded close to perfect, if slightly intimidating. The job would put me in charge of programming at Hallmark Entertainment, which had seventeen channels and an international audience of fifty million viewers. I was nervous about moving to a new country, the biggest entertainment pond on the planet, with two babies in tow. There were plenty of reasons to find a more comfortable arrangement to curl up with. But Denver struck me as family friendly, and the opportunity to gain experience in the international cable market and expand the skill set I had been growing for a decade outweighed my apprehension. And I wasn't wrong.

At Trio, I had a clear mandate to broaden the audience base and shake up the status quo. At Hallmark, my role was essentially mine to create. When I arrived in Denver, the networks' schedules were geared toward airing the shows in the Hallmark Hall of Fame Library, a rich repository of programs and television movies stretching back to the 1950s. But the lineups tended to have little to do with the interests of its international audience. In fact, a recent Employee of the Month had been lauded for finding a way to maximize the number of times a show could be broadcast by using a program that worked out the run dates and spaced out the repeats. It was called a "schedulizer," and was designed to benefit the company as rights holder over the viewer. The audience didn't factor into it at all. The *Oldest Living Confederate Widow Tells All* just doesn't mean much to people watching in Australia or Japan, for instance. But no one wants to hear, especially from the new boss, that they are pursuing the wrong definition of success and serving the company's narrowest interest.

So I told these employees that their approach was important in maximizing the benefits from the rights we held, but I suggested that they could create a bigger business picture by serving, even potentially building, audiences where we had them. I commissioned research to understand our viewer base, research that informed the way we redesigned our schedule. There would be no more one-schedule-fits-all and no more being only a movie channel. We picked up the broadcast rights to *Star Trek* in Asia, where research showed audiences were keen on the old-school sci-fi series. For women in Latin America, who reported that they often watched television while they did household chores like ironing, we featured the emotional dramas they said they enjoyed.

Every tweak to the lineup represented a departure from what the company had been doing—and a risk. But they'd hired me, an outsider, which indicated that management was ready to take risks.

By its nature, television is all about taking risks: you select a show and invest in its development and have no real idea if it will succeed until after it goes to air. Since many shows do fail, you have to live in that space that drives accountants crazy. They always want to know how many will fail—two shows out of ten? Five out of ten? By contrast, as the person in charge, I had to allow for the possibility of failure. If you never fail it means you are never trying anything new. Success means you've made more right decisions than wrong ones, but you can't let failure define you. Making a big generalization here, but Canadians tend to be risk-averse, too worried that we are only as good as the last thing we did. Whereas in the States, the emphasis was not on what you'd done that had worked or failed, but what you were going to do next. At Hallmark, I learned to be less intimidated by failure, because failure was not cast in the same devastating light as it was back home.

Over three and a half years, we built a wide and diverse international audience, which made Hallmark Entertainment yet another attractive property, and eventually, it was sold. But even before that happened, I knew it was time to go home. It was just after 9/11, which had deeply affected my colleagues, and not only in our New York office. My oldest daughter was just about to start grade school and I was tired of not getting to eat Shreddies. But with every job that followed, I carried a little bit of that American-daring sensibility with me. In 2003, when I became the senior vice-president of programming for the Alliance Atlantis specialty channels, the experience I'd gleaned at Hallmark allowed me to do what I felt needed to be done, and that meant shaking things up.

The job involved responsibility for programming the broadcaster's lifestyle channels, which were in need of renovation. A lot of the shows were of the strictly instructional variety: how to plan a party, set the dinner table, plant begonias. But as I'd already seen in the US, reality-based shows that told a story as they imparted information were gaining real traction with audiences keen not only to learn, but to learn while being entertained. Tastes were changing and we needed to get ahead of the audience. Not long after I arrived, I heard a pitch from the team for a show from a contractor named Mike Holmes that seemed to fit this bill perfectly. At the time, Mike had been featured on CTV doing lunchtime news break how-to segments. But he saw potential in recasting himself as a kind of vigilante contractor, the big guy who comes in to nail the crooked contractor who wrecked your home with shoddy installation or substandard plumbing that flooded your basement.

I was intrigued by the drama he was selling. For most people, their homes are the biggest—perhaps the only—investment they'll ever make. Then someone comes along and takes advantage of their efforts to make improvements and puts their greatest asset at risk. This was real-life drama. If Holmes could rescue them from that fate, he was more like a white knight than a vigilante. That tweak to the concept made *Holmes on Homes* something unique in the home-improvement genre, a show that wouldn't just demonstrate how to repair a broken tile, but would tug at viewers' hearts.

The team was nervous. Personality-driven narrative was a risky venture. Building a whole show around a relatively unknown guy was not a safe bet. And building a show around one person whose name was in the title was asking for it. What if viewers didn't like Mike Holmes? The show would die. If we pulled it off, he'd become a celebrity and could leave the network for the big time someplace else. Building him into a star would give him power the networks were reluctant to share. Talent was considered safest when it remained nameless and faceless, and therefore interchangeable. But not taking this risk meant passing up on the potential of great reward. As I had learned, sharing power and investing it in others comes back with big dividends.

I decided that Mike Holmes needed to be front and centre. And who would pass up a title like *Holmes on Homes?* No one else on TV looked like him—this big strapping man with a buzz cut and overalls. Mike had the perfect look to play a white-knight character, and I was sure the show would be a hit; the possibility that its popularity would ultimately cost us Holmes sounded like a short-sighted reason not to try. If we cultivated a trusting relationship and committed to supporting Holmes's development, he'd have every reason to stay. In the end, it was my call and my risk to take, and I took it, knowing I had spotted "it" in Mike Holmes and I didn't want to let it get away.

There's been a sea of ink spilled on the way leaders, and women in particular, regard risk-taking. Most of it has cast women as being almost biologically risk-averse, genetically driven to cautiously mind the cave and pick berries with babes strapped to our backs. According to the evolutionary stereotypes, we weren't out hunting and confronting death at every turn, so what do we know from risk? It's a bias about the real nature of women that media and popular culture have spun into the contemporary workplace. Some studies have even considered whether the global financial crisis of 2008 could have been averted if more women than cowboys had been in charge. But there's real danger in putting stock in prehistoric depictions that suggest women, by nature, are prone to play it safe, because the characterization can become a self-fulfilling prophecy. The hard fact is that females are socialized to be restrained. Even before girls go to preschool, they've ingested the cultural expectation that good girls sit still and behave, and they're rewarded when they do just that. This is why so many girls are at the head of the class.

But in the business world, that mode of the behaviour is the ball and chain we have to sever to succeed. And there is lots of evidence that we're making that break. The trouble is that for too long the very term "risk" has been defined in masculine terms, both physical and financial, as though risk-taking is simply about going brave with biceps and piles of cash. But in the workplace, a risk is any situation that carries the potential for negative consequences. Any time I changed a program lineup, altered a schedule or chose to invest in a new show, I was taking a risk, especially if there was opposition. The risk was not just that ratings would suffer if I made the wrong decision, but that my credibility as a leader was on the line. Failure in my job was public.

Increasingly, researchers are recognizing that there's more than one kind of risk, that men and women tend to perceive risk differently and that when you take these distinctions into account, you actually find that the old saw about women being risk-averse is mostly a steaming hill of myth. If girls have been brought up with expectations of being seen but not heard, boys have learned that boyish behaviour includes pushing boundaries and breaking rules. All grown up, men tend to define risks in terms of the visible, as in betting the farm or bungee jumping. Women, on the other hand, are more apt to define risk in terms of the invisible, as in taking a position that puts your personal capital on the line. Often, that includes the sense that there's a risk to speaking up—as in raising your voice, if not your hand.

That's not just my take, that's at the core of the more recent explorations into gender and risk-taking. A 2012 Tufts University study, for instance, backed by the Institute for New Thinking in Economics, reviewed 28 papers on the subject and found that the gender differences around risk-taking have been exaggerated. A survey of 650 female managers by the Simmons School of Management in Boston found about 80 percent of the women reported regularly taking risks in their professional lives around things like pursuing a major change initiative, or new programs, but that these pursuits are not recognized as risk-taking in part because of societal expectations that women are risk-averse. Columbia Business School's report in 2011 concluded that both sexes are equally risk-prone, but in different ways. Simply put: men took more risks with money, women with social situations, a category that included things like launching a new career in your mid-thirties and sharing an unpopular opinion in a work meeting. And finally, there's the added nuance of context. As a recent

Wall Street Journal article explained it, using the example of a conservative money manager who likes to ride the fastest motorcycle on the highway in his off-hours: even the cautious can become daredevils in the right context. Today's context demands that everyone be at least a little daredevil.

In the digital age, leaders need to innovate constantly, moving in directions no one has ever has gone before. Everything is risky. We are living in the time of the unorthodox. In many ways, women are primed to take advantage of that unorthodoxy because our mere presence as leaders is still so novel that it instantly signals a new approach—as it did for the young women I met in the halls of the CBC. The same Caliper study that profiled the gender differences in modern leadership strengths, for instance, found that women leaders are more likely to push back against established ways of doing things, because women are more likely to view them as "old rules"—stale dictates from a bygone day that are holding back progress. It also concluded that women tend to act with urgency in changing the old ways and coming up with innovative solutions, perhaps because, as I learned in my career, our credibility and future effectiveness as leaders depends on it.

From Paragon right through to Twitter, I've always been less interested in what has been than what could be. My own sense of urgency comes in part from realizing that taking the right risk, with the right result, has a major impact on my personal capital. If I am going to be an effective leader, I have to be seen and trusted to lead effectively. I have so often been the newcomer, the underestimated young blonde brought in to shake things up, that if I don't move quickly and notch up items in the win column, I soon won't be able to lead at all.

And that was the story at Alliance Atlantis as well. Sure, it would have been easier to make yet another how-to gardening show, but in the end developing *Holmes on Homes*— despite the risks—not only produced a hit and a homegrown celebrity, it helped to invigorate the HGTV brand in Canada and bring it fame and success in the US. With a new lineup of personality-driven shows and reality-based narratives (which included creating household names like Sarah Richardson, Michael Smith and the Designer Guys), we started a trend. We weren't buying our hits from the US, they were buying from us. And soon after, the CBC sought me out. Talk about an interesting job for someone who had embraced being a risk-taker.

In her book *Stop Playing Safe*, Australian author Margie Warrell writes that the more chances people take, the less they overestimate negative consequences and the more comfortable they become with taking chances, or as she put it in an interview, "The more often we step out of our comfort zone, the more we build our tolerance for risk-taking." I can attest to the wisdom of that.

Slipping into Something Uncomfortable

ON PAPER, TAKING A JOB AT the Canadian Broadcasting Corporation seemed like a mad thing to consider. At Alliance Atlantis, I was sailing a sturdy ship on a sea of high ratings and revenues. I worked with an amazing, invigorated team. Why would I leave it to become programming chief at the embattled CBC, facing challenges that pundits described as Herculean—probably one of the most thankless posts in the broadcast world. Why would I swap my comfy perch for a hot seat?

In the fall of 2014, I moderated a panel discussion at a symposium for Women in Payments, an organization that represents females working in finance. Sitting on the stage were eight successful female CEOs and entrepreneurs describing their experiences and trading insights on how women in the workplace can get ahead. As I looked out at the room full of women who had come to hear their stories, I asked myself what it was that distinguished these women up onstage. As the discussion continued, I realized the common link that united us: at one time or another, each of us had pushed ourselves to take a position that was not only unfamiliar, but a deliberate plunge into the decidedly *uncomfortable*.

Whether it was taking a job with a perpendicular learning curve or walking away from the security of a steady paycheque to strike out on one's own, we had all of us taken a chance on a professional opportunity that cast us far out of our comfort zones. These zones are the *mind states* we occupy when our ability to do a job well becomes so effortless that it outweighs any anxiety about actually doing the job. It's generally low-risk and stress-free. There are times in a career when the comfort zone job is precisely what you need—when havoc breaks out in your personal life or you're hatching entrepreneurial plans while carrying on with a day job. But I have always felt that comfort-zone jobs invariably lead to boredom and restlessness. Stepping into an uncomfortable zone can be scary, but it also can be a wild and exhilarating ride driven by raw curiosity—your own. There's a curiosity about the job itself, but also about whether you have the stuff to do it.

Did the CBC sound like a daunting challenge? You bet. Even as I went through the lengthy run of one-on-one and panel interviews, I continued to turn over the pros and cons of actually taking the job. Ultimately, the words of a good friend silenced my concerns. Donna Bevelander, an executive at Alliance Atlantis who had once headed up media operations at CBC, told me that it would be a tough job, with too many masters, and a massive bureaucracy notoriously inhospitable to women. But, she said, it was also a place teeming with some of the smartest people in the country, and that it was the biggest sandbox I would ever play in. That was the point that was irresistible to me. But I wouldn't have wanted to play in that sandbox if I thought there was nothing I could bring to the job.

I'D LIKE TO THINK THAT the goal of engaging the audience was the hallmark of my four-year run as head of television programming at the CBC. Not everything worked. There were shows I commissioned that never made it to air and others that were cancelled. I faced philosophical challenges of "whither the CBC." But there was something to learn from every setback and failure. And there were certainly more wins than losses. I was proud of the evolution I was steering and utterly humbled by the hard-working teams who pushed to remake the broadcaster into the successful media company I knew it could be. When Richard Stursberg left the top job in 2010, my fellow senior execs at CBC lobbied Hubert Lacroix, the network's politically appointed president, to make me Stursberg's successor. I'm sure their support had something to do with me being "the devil they knew," but I believe they also felt that I had put the CBC on a good path.

We had proved to the country, and ourselves, that we could produce a string of smart and popular shows. We won back the broadcasting rights to the Olympics from CTV and Rogers, and even as groups within the CBC argued that no one would ever watch TV on a computer, let alone a smartphone, we expanded our digital offerings so viewers could access our news and programming any-where, anytime, through cbcnews, cbc.ca and CBC Music (a digital music service started under my watch that pro-vides online streaming of more than fifty-three web radio services, including forty-seven devoted to specific music genres). They were initiatives I hoped set us on a path to modernize the network.

In January 2011, I was officially named executive vice-president of CBC's English-language services and in that first year we were making real progress. But, suddenly, prog-ress came to a grinding halt. In March 2012, the government announced it was cutting our budget by 10 percent—$115 million over three years. It was difficult to digest the pain we were facing. Such a budget cut meant nearly 200 hours of programming we could no longer produce. It meant the can-cellation of several shows and doling out more repeats. Worst of all, at least 650 people were about to lose their jobs. As awful as it was for me to contemplate how I could do my job with such cuts coming, it was nothing compared to the impact on the many fine people about to be let go.

What made it all the worse was that I had pushed everyone to work hard for change under the logical assumption that their work would be rewarded. Every triumph we'd achieved had represented the sweat of many; I'd maintained that if we pulled together and reached certain milestones, the future would be brighter. Everyone had done exactly that. Ratings were up. Revenues were up. And now we were to be squeezed despite our success.

I'd heard that the last time a CBC executive had announced a round of cuts, people had rushed the stage and someone had thrown a chair in disgust. I expected to meet a similar fate. I stood on a brightly lit stage in front of the Toronto staff—with the announcement being beamed into CBC offices across the country—and told them the bad news. They knew it was coming. The signs had been there for days, and they were anxious to hear what it meant for them. I explained how we would deal with the cuts, the values on which decisions were to be made and what our priorities for investment would be moving forward. I couldn't sugar-coat it. I wasn't vague. I was too distraught to serve them anything but the straight goods; and they'd earned that honesty. I was moved to tears, but my own feelings didn't matter. At the end of the day, many of them wouldn't have a job—but I still would. I felt sadness, mixed with guilt, and with anger of my own.

And I expected to face anger. It would have been justified. Instead, I was met with resignation: we tried, we succeeded, but some things are out of our control. We would keep trying. The most touching moment happened after I left the stage and stepped into an elevator. A young man, whose new job at the CBC was most certainly disappearing, turned to me and said, "Ms. Stewart, I want to shake your hand." He told me he thought my job was very complicated, but that no boss had ever shared the inside story around how the tough decisions would be made. He said he had never felt so respected in such a devastating moment. It was a generous gift he offered me at a time when he could have chosen to be angry. And it's a moment that I'll always have as a reminder of the value of trusting people with the truth. They will trust you back. The days of controlling the message are so over.

THAT DAY MARKED THE BEGINNING of the end for me at the CBC. As I went on to implement the cuts, and at the same time roll out an ambitious plan for our Sochi Olympics coverage, I could see that the broadcaster was in serious danger of becoming a symbol of all that was wrong with old media. We had been able to take some risks and invest in innovation because we'd had the success of the new prime-time programming to build from. But now, it was all in danger of entering a death spiral. The balance was always tenuous as we tried to keep the seventy-five-year-old CBC on the side of the new and the different. But now, with not enough to go around even to maintain the status quo, old habits and battles resurfaced. Many felt let down by the CBC president, Hubert Lacroix, who had been unable and, some argued, unwilling to fight with his political masters for the stability of the public broadcaster over which he presided.

The end of the end came on a busy street corner in New York City in the winter of 2012. I had just emerged from another friendly meeting with National Hockey League commissioner Gary Bettman, who was himself leading the NHL through difficult times. (The landscape was changing dramatically for both broadcasters and league, and I knew our budget would leave us little room for negotiating a renewal of our hockey rights. I met with him to lay the groundwork to try to hold on to some version of CBC's most lucrative show, *Hockey Night in Canada*.) My phone buzzed with a text from an insider in CBC news, letting me know that Hubert Lacroix had just had his tenure renewed as CBC's president and CEO. It was as if the stop sign that loomed above my head on Fifth Avenue called to me. Nothing was going to change, when all around the media market, change was everywhere. Lacroix's renewal signalled a status quo I couldn't live with anymore. I decided to leave my job.

Leading the CBC would no longer be about applying my strengths to meet the shifting demands of the new market. My mandate going forward would be more administrative, less aspirational. I couldn't look ahead and lead a team where success was no promise of reward, where wins wouldn't necessarily earn us reinvestment, and where people could be punished, not praised, for doing their best work. Spending my days trying to figure out how to keep a big ship afloat with half a paddle wasn't for me. I found nothing honest or inspiring about it. I had been at the CBC for nearly seven years at that point, and while I'd never describe it as a comfort zone, it was no longer a zone I could inhabit comfortably. I could imagine a CBC, post-cuts, that would focus on its strengths, such as news and what mattered most to Canadians. But there were too many masters to serve and they weren't ready for the wholesale change that had to come. In that environment, I had nothing left to offer. It was time for me to go.

But it wasn't just about leaving the CBC. It was my exit from an entire industry whose time at the top was waning and whose leadership seemed to lack the courage to chart an effective way forward. I may have been doing one of the most important jobs in Canadian television, but what was television becoming? It was already clear that advertisers would soon be spending more on online digital ads than they would on print, radio and TV (a milestone surpassed in Canada in 2013, and a year later in the United States). So while other large traditional media organizations sent attractive offers my way, I was already sold on a new direction. The promise and potential of a new view of media hooked me. Technology was giving power to the very people I had made a career serving—those glorious masses. And I wanted to hear what they had to say.

IV

You Need to Get
Over Yourself

AT TWITTER HEADQUARTERS IN San Francisco, the staff
gathers every week for Tea Time. It's a casual end-of-day
event, beer and wine along with the tea, held in the wide-open
space of the company lounge with added chairs and a stage
up front. People make presentations about specific projects
or new directions and employees chime in with comments
and questions. But not all employees spoke up. Last year, the
company's SWAT team noticed that relatively few of the Tea
Time questions were coming from women. Short for Super
Women at Twitter, SWAT is the cheekily named internal
team that works to advance women's interests at the company. I became part of the team not long after I joined Twitter
in the spring of 2013. I've always believed that advocating for
women in the workplace requires a constant, concerted effort.
Tea Time was a case in point. Here was a regular opportunity
for employees to be heard, yet too many of the women who
came out to the sessions stayed silent.

Like many of the big tech and social networking companies, Twitter has more men than women among its three thousand or so employees. So proportionally, one would expect to hear from more men at any company forum. But I know too well that numbers don't tell the whole story. Even when there are more women than men in a group, or at the table, there's no guarantee you'll hear from them. Stacks of evidence show women are far less likely than men to speak up in the workplace. And when women are outnumbered by men, they're even more inclined to keep their thoughts to themselves. In 2012, researchers at Brigham Young University and Princeton examined how groups that included men and women collaborated to solve problems. They found that when women were in the minority they not only spoke less than the men, they spoke significantly less than their proportional representation might suggest: in those cases, females talked for less than 75 percent of the time that males did.

The finding is no surprise to me. In my experience, when men and women gather for a work meeting a remarkable ritual often unfolds. Perhaps because the boardroom table was historically the domain of men, an ancient, almost tribal dynamic takes hold. The men jostle and posture. They speak freely and unprompted. They interrupt each other, often talking over one another, talking over the woman. I have been that woman. I've been the one who has offered up an idea, only to have it drowned out and then hear it repeated almost word for word a minute later by, say, John. This then cues Richard to say, "John makes an excellent point!" And while I seethe in silence, the men move into mid-ritual, reinforcing and reframing each other's views. Like a game, they toss a ball of ideas around the table, and flex their personal capital.

Women are still newcomers to this game. And while we can be terrific at reading a room, we don't always read it well in such moments. We're too stumped by being talked over, or having our idea hijacked, to join in. Yet it's in those moments, like it or not, that you have to get over yourself and jump in. Bringing an idea to the table doesn't mean you "own" it. The team owns it, adds to it, debates it, fleshes it out. If you have a great idea, set it free; if you hear a good idea, back it up and bring additional value to it. The meeting table isn't a place to go it alone, but a place where you anchor yourself as part of a team.

Yet it isn't easy, and we women don't get over ourselves enough. We fall back on another traditional pattern, reminiscent of the classroom, when you put your hand up and waited to be called upon (reinforced by what you've seen happen to the woman who speaks first). And while you wait, you formulate precisely what you want to say, only to find that when it's your "turn," you have missed the moment or someone else already has made the point. Fretting over saying just the right thing and fearing saying the wrong thing, women can end up saying nothing at all.

I know this particular insecurity intimately. Having so often been the newbie, the only woman and/or the youngest exec at the table, I have felt so out of place it robbed me of my voice. I was shy, too careful about what I'd say, or how I'd say it. More than once, my bosses told me during performance reviews that they felt that I knew more than I was contributing.

Women do not have a lock on being shy. Men suffer too. Strangely, given my chosen career, I have no desire to be at a podium. I take a deep breath before presenting my ideas and making jokes in front of large crowds of people. But it's my job. And if I'm going to do my job well, I have to pull myself together and contribute.

In the workplace, I've been able to overcome shyness by defining it for what it is—a kind of self-indulgence. To be shy or too quiet in work situations means you hide who you are, and, more significantly, hide what you think and what you know. By not speaking up, you don't just deprive yourself of a voice at the table, you also abdicate contributing to the group. And that means you're actually not doing your job. After all, if you've been asked to the table in the first place, your colleagues and your bosses believe you have something valuable to contribute. The invitation is to participate and by taking that seat, you have accepted. When people don't share to their full potential, the group loses out—particularly in these times. As the digital age prompts widespread downsizing, every voice matters. It's not just the views of the leader that are critical, but those of every member of the team. The cards you keep close to the vest might well be the answer to a problem, or a map of the best way forward.

Or maybe you're afraid your input could be rejected or your suggestion isn't good enough. Sure, the chance is always there that you might say something that will make others question your judgement or abilities. And, unfortunately, women are still vulnerable to the knee-jerk judgements of others. Stereotypes are powerful, and stubborn old cultural views about how a woman ought to look/think/act are hard to shake. A 2012 Yale University study found women who speak their minds are still seen as both overbearing and less competent than their quieter peers, while outspoken men are viewed as more competent than their quieter colleagues—and they tend to be rewarded for it. In the workplace, the talkative male tends to be seen as confident and powerful while an assertive woman runs the risk of being labelled bossy, domineering and, yes, bitchy. So it's worth noting that women's fears around speaking up are not unfounded. But staying quiet is not the solution. If those damaging, limiting perspectives are to change, men and women have to stop buying into them. We don't do ourselves any favours when we do.

So what if when you step up for your moment in the spotlight you say something wrong? In reality, your thoughts drop into the conversation and the team moves on, whether you've been brilliant or not. I had to ask myself, "Just how important do I think I am that my words have that kind of staying power?" You may ruminate in the shower or lose sleep over some stupid thing you think you said, but in those situations there are very few mistakes that can't be forgiven, and usually they are so small that they're quickly forgotten. Looking at it that way convinced me I was holding myself back—and, frankly, not doing my job when I sat quiet in a meeting. It was wrong *not* to speak up. In the end I decided I just had to get over myself.

At the CBC, I made a point of putting my views forward within the organization, but I also tried to make my voice heard outside of it. It was crucial to recasting the network as a modern broadcaster with clout. In 2011, when the Ontario Teachers' Pension Plan sold its majority stake in Maple Leaf Sports and Entertainment to Rogers Communications and Bell Media (BCE), who as a result became owners of the

Maple Leafs hockey team. I was concerned the public might interpret the deal to mean that the CBC no longer had the rights to broadcast the Leafs' games. To establish publicly that the CBC hadn't lost anything, I put out a statement congratulating Bell and Rogers on the deal, and said that we at the CBC—as the home of the Maple Leafs on *Hockey Night in Canada*—looked forward to working with them. Speaking up brought me an insult from a prominent Canadian sportswriter who published a column saying I was "blowing kisses to the boys."

I was grateful Twitter had been invented. It allowed me to speak up again, and instantly. I tweeted the writer's misogynistic comment and asked whether this was still 1952. The tweet echoed far and wide, as men and women re-tweeted it with a heavy dose of disdain for the backward attitude.

The incident was one of many that taught me that you can't withdraw from criticism. You have to resist the temptation to give in to insecurities and allow others to define you. If you have a point to make, or you're doing something you believe is for the greater good, you have to just do it, ignoring the risk that a few might call you out and disagree. By not speaking up you run a greater risk of being misjudged. As I like to advise people who are hesitant to join Twitter, people are going to talk about you anyways—wouldn't you rather be part of the conversation? To cede the floor is to let others speak about you and, worse, speak on your behalf. I think our tendency to keep our heads down and just get on with our work can be one of the barriers that keep women from getting ahead—but it's one that is within our power to overcome. The keep-your-head-down attitude might win good girls praise in school, but the business world will punish you for it. That's not to say that you should suddenly become a blowhard or magically transform from wallflower to show-off. But if you have an interesting observation, share it. If you have an idea, present it. You have to lift your head up every now and again. You have to get over yourself to be yourself.

Speaking up doesn't guarantee results. I learned that hard lesson dealing with a group of comedy writers who worked on shows commissioned by the CBC. Some of those guys, and they were all guys, had been working with the broadcaster for years, and as I made a push toward including more shows with female leads, I read some scripts that compelled me to speak up. In one episode, they had the female character, a newly single woman, diving under a table in a restaurant to hide when her ex walks in. In another, the lonely dumped woman was holed up eating ice cream in her closet. When I pointed out that these were clichés, they told me that their wives thought they were funny. They gave me the distinct impression that I, that women, weren't even allowed in this work area of funny men. We added women to writers' rooms but then got feedback from many of those women that they were being ignored. And they were too intimidated in a transient career to go on the record with their complaints. One pregnant network exec told me she'd felt ridiculed. As the network boss all I could do was keep returning to check that writers' room out and keep tabs on the creative process, though from an increased distance as the boys circled their wagons. We were hoping to broaden the primetime audience and appeal to more women and younger women, in particular, and they were still mining old boys' humour for laughs.

I not only had every right to give them my input, it was my job to do so. I never did break through that wall. I failed. But I never stopped trying to make myself heard—and that really is the crux of it.

The more I forced myself to speak up—to speak out, to question, to muse—the more comfortable it became. Practice was the best behavioural training. Not that it was always easy. But if you don't use your voice, it atrophies. With regular exercise it gets stronger. That strength is crucial not just for those who lead, but for any woman who hopes to make a meaningful contribution at work.

No, We Haven't Come a Long Way—Not Yet

EVER SINCE I STARTED AT PARAGON, I have belonged to organizations that work to help women exercise their voice in the workplace and keep our interests showing up on corporate agendas. I've been a member of Toronto Women in Film, Women in Communications, and a number of internal groups that advocate for women's issues within a company. I think it's dangerous to assume we've come far enough, as many women and men actually seem to do. The reality is that business is not doing well enough by women yet. It may be tempting to say, "Okay, we've ticked that box" after one or two women are hired to senior roles and as a result become the poster faces of female progress. This tiny minority of female leaders, wearing heels among all those men in brogues, are presented as living examples of the success of the women's movement. But only a slim fraction of corporate leaders are female and, in the ranks below, the situation may not be much better. Even in the tech industry, where women have made noted inroads at the highest levels, more than two-thirds of employees are male.

At the CBC, I instituted a diversity plan to make sure we kept asking the question "Where are the women? Where's the diversity?" Reporting directly to me, its director had a mandate to analyze who was doing the job on camera and behind the scenes. Just making that effort to count and question made people pay attention to the composition of a group and how they could affect it by their own recruitment and casting decisions. It wasn't about meeting quotas. It was about staying mindful and trying to correct imbalances where they existed.

Today, social media is ushering in a whole a new level of mindfulness to these kinds of issues. Through blogs, websites and social networks, ever more instances of imbalance, injustice, discrimination, both subtle and overt, are called out online in a digital recast of feminist activism. It's massive, hyper-organized and seems to move almost at the speed of sound.

It's true there's a dichotomy: in the online space, women and girls are easily stalked, threatened and bullied by anonymous creeps. But it's also an open space where people can share, support one another and discuss the kinds of issues—like sexism at work, domestic violence and date rape—that were once only talked about anonymously and in whispers. It's an intimate conversation among the masses, making women feel less alone, if not empowered. Granted, there's no pretense of a united female voice here: there may be nearly as many battlegrounds between women as there are around them (left vs. right, east vs. west, black vs. white; all the iterations of the mommy wars). But there's no denying that social media have created a new power to force change.

Just ask Rush Limbaugh. After the ultra-conservative radio host called former Georgetown University Law student Sandra Fluke a "slut" and a "prostitute" for asking the government to cover the costs of birth control at a congressional hearing in 2012, the online protest ignited by his rant is still burning three years later: the public outrage that went viral prompted several sponsors to pull ads from his show, consumers to boycott advertisers who hadn't pulled their ads, and national advertisers to boycott the show itself. Or consider the amazing effect of a protest campaign started by one teenager. Julia Bluhm, a fourteen-year-old from Maine, started an online petition at Change.org, entitled "*Seventeen* Magazine: Give Girls Images of Real Girls!" Some 84,000 people signed it, which in turn led to a protest that convinced *Seventeen* magazine to introduce a Body Peace Treaty that promises to "never change girls' body or face shapes" when retouching images. That treaty, aimed at reducing the self-esteem problems and skyrocketing cases of eating disorders among teenage girls, has since been policed online by people who post any perceived breaches.

No other kind of activism in history can rally as many as quickly as social media can, virtually speaking. It's fostering a society of whistleblowers, because the web gives everyone a whistle. Neither power, nor powerful friends, fame nor money can escape the matrix of social media. Online, status does not have its privileges. Just ask running back Ray Rice, fired from the Baltimore Ravens and suspended from the NFL after footage of him punching out his then fiancée in an elevator went viral. Ask Bill Cosby. Ask Jian Ghomeshi. Months before the mainstream media broke the story, a Twitter account was accusing the former CBC radio host of sexual violence.

I was in the midst of working on this book when I learned, along with most of the world, that Ghomeshi, whose arts and entertainment show, *Q*, had more than two million listeners and syndication in more than 160 US markets, had allegedly used his celebrity to sexually abuse women and mistreat his staff. As of this writing, Ghomeshi awaits trial on five charges of sexual assault plus one charge related to overcoming resistance by choking. The disturbing news, gushing forth as it did over several weeks last fall, was hard to fathom. Several nights I lay awake wondering how I'd heard nothing about this aspect of Ghomeshi's behaviour. If I had, I wouldn't have hesitated to act and act quickly, as I have done throughout my career when people have mistreated or been inappropriate with those working with them. It upset me to discover that there were places within that five-thousand-person environment where people felt they couldn't come to me. I wish they had. But I also completely understand why some might have felt that they couldn't: reporting puts a lot of responsibility on the victim, often too much. I know that first-hand. My first brush was at the age of twenty, when a boss of mine openly propositioned me on my first business trip. I kept quiet. I reminded myself every day, as many young women do, that I was lucky to have the job, that I was replaceable and that anyone would kill to take my place. According to Statistics Canada, 90 percent of sex assaults go unreported. And that's been one of the remarkable side effects of the Ghomeshi story, seeing and hearing the many women who now feel empowered to speak up through social media in numbers that have made the mainstream press and society at large pay attention. When Canadian actress Lucy DeCoutere became the first woman to put her name to her allegations against Ghomeshi, the story went live on the *Toronto Star* website at 9:35 p.m. and, according to a *Chatelaine* investigation by Rachel Giese, within half an hour #IBelieveLucy had more than 2,000 mentions and 2.5 million impressions online. Along with that came the support of other women who had stayed silent for so long, culminating in #BeenRapedNeverReported, the hashtag launched on Twitter by Canadian journalists Sue Montgomery and Antonia Zerbisias, which went viral within a day of its creation. From my perspective, it's all evidence that the digital universe can tip the scales in favour of what's right: enabling women, no matter who they are, where they are, or what the context, to find their voice.

Why Reaching Critical Mass Is Critical

IT WAS DURING ONE OF the regular Twitter SWAT team conference calls that one of the members said she had noticed that too few females were speaking up at Tea Time. We discussed why this might be the case, and what we could do about it and, in the end, we decided that perhaps more women would feel encouraged to speak up if other women did. And so we decided to encourage selected women to break the ice and step forward with questions. It had an amazing result. More women did start speaking up, either inspired by hearing the voices of other women or deciding they needed to follow their example. Either way, women regularly now step up to the microphone at Tea Time.

Why go to such an effort? It's not just about pushing females forward. It's about doing what's truly good for everyone. Getting input from diverse voices, people of different ages, cultures and experience, has always been valuable. But in the information age, it's urgent and critical. There's just so much data flying around, no one leader, or narrow management team, can possibly keep abreast of it, let alone analyze and exploit it to a company's advantage. A recent article in the *Harvard Business Review*, for example, suggests that one of the reasons one-time telecom giant Nokia failed was the homogeneity of its executive team. One hundred percent Finnish and together for more than a decade, the team completely underestimated the threat of the smartphone from Silicon Valley. The Center for Talent Innovation, based on survey responses from 1,800 men and women in white-collar professions and dozens of interviews with Fortune 500 executives and staff, found that the failure to innovate is often a reflection of senior management's homogeneity (53 percent of respondents said leadership at their firms was almost entirely white, or almost entirely male). Homogeneity as a liability is a message now making a major impression in the business world, and the trick for the modern leader is how to create this new kind of eclectic, speak-up culture.

The point is that increasing the diversity of voices in the workplace can mean the difference between success and failure. Homogeneity is a creativity killer. And several studies, from various countries, suggest that having more women in leadership roles, whether it is in management, the C-suite or on corporate boards, the more successful companies tend to be. Part of the difficulty in making this case is that there are far too few women at the very top of anything to make a statistically powerful argument. But the research is all telling us the same thing. The McKinsey & Co. *Women Matter* report, for example, finds that companies with the highest level of gender diversity in top management roles outperform their sector in terms of return on equity, operations and stock price. What's more, when the global consulting firm assessed the organizational excellence of companies on nine criteria, which included things like leadership, direction, innovation, coordination, capability and values, it found that firms with three or more women in senior management scored more highly on every measure. And organizational excellence, no surprise, is a key indicator of financial success. But what's really worth noting is that these companies—101 of them around the world along with survey answers from more than 58,000 respondents—only saw this effect when they had three women or more at the top. Yet further proof that numbers matter, and that there's a darn good business reason to do more than nudge them up by a token one or two.

In 2004, Catalyst, the international non-profit group that aims to advance women's opportunities in business, also found that firms with the *highest* representation of women on their top management teams performed better financially than those companies with the lowest female representation across each of five industries studied. Catalyst based its research on two key financial measures: return on equity, which was 35 percent higher in companies with more women in senior posts, and total returns to shareholders, which was

34 percent higher. Then, just a few years later, in 2011, Catalyst released a study showing that companies with high numbers of female board directors outperformed those with lower numbers by 16 percent, based on return on sales. That number jumped to 26 percent when comparing companies with the highest representation of female board directors to those firms with the fewest.

The financial benefits of female leadership are also gaining global recognition. Researchers from Milan's Bocconi University and the University of Barcelona produced a groundbreaking study in 2014 that found that medium to large family businesses in Italy were more successful when they had more women at the helm. (The researchers said they focused on family firms because they represented the most common ownership form worldwide, even among large publicly traded US companies. According to their data, families hold large equity stakes in about a third of S&P 500 firms, and half of the two thousand largest industrial firms.) The study found that replacing a family firm's male CEO with a female increased profitability. But the increase was most dramatic when that change was also coupled with an increase in the number of female board members, jumping by about 18 percent and making female-led firms more profitable than those with all-male boards. The combination of female leadership and governance, the researchers said, encouraged a kind of cooperation and rich information exchange that improved the quality of the board's advice and the performance of the CEO.

It's an observation that lends hefty support to the importance of female input at the highest levels but also of cooperation in modern enterprise. The time has come for companies to revamp the way they operate and move away from top-down-driven leadership. When companies are smaller, and team members multi-task, and there's a daily feast of data to be digested, collaboration and consensus is simply the smart way forward. And years of research show that women have an edge in forming collaborative relationships. In the scenarios where consensus is the goal, females also seem to naturally find their voice. The study from Brigham and Princeton, for instance, which found that women speak less than men in group problem-solving situations, discovered that the disparity vanished when the group was asked to come to a unanimous decision. In other words, when a group was required to build consensus instead of allowing the majority to rule, women felt empowered to speak up even if they were outnumbered by men.

Given that collaboration is proving so essential to modern leadership, businesses need to create environments that foster broad input and brainstorming. They have to move away from hierarchies toward a culture of openness where everyone has a voice. And for men and women who tend to excel in these kinds of environments, the time is ripe for women to play to those strengths in the boardroom and beyond. The trick for the modern leader is how to create this new kind of culture.

The Power of the Outsider

BEFORE I LANDED AT THE CBC, I lived through a variety of management styles. There were places, such as Paragon under Isme Bennie, where initiative was encouraged and rewarded. And I knew, from my own meteoric rise there, that the business as a whole benefits when the leader gains a broad perspective from the team, and that leaders are only as effective as the team they build.

The trouble was the CBC was facing many of the same structural issues as any seventy-year-old company. It was a model of big bureaucracy, with many departments and many divisions with more separation between them than I had ever seen—real silos in which the leaders were deeply entrenched and distrustful of others. It was like a collection of tiny empires rather than any kind of cohesive unit. Not that they were at war with one another, but they certainly didn't cooperate much. When I ran television we had nothing to do with radio, the radio team had nothing to do with digital, and so on.

The experience of the CBC's digital group was a good example of what was going on in the culture. Launched when digital was seen as a niche inhabited only by the tech savvy, the digital group occupied its own separate division, a place for "special projects." The digital landscape was swiftly evolving and reaching into all departments even as the division itself was growing up separately, struggling steadily with the broadcaster's competing priorities. As a result, digital had created its own shadow departments, digital people who worked specifically in each of these areas—duplicating efforts, hampering good communication and stunting innovation. People outside digital were confused by its mandate. If they were asked to produce web content, they'd reply: "That's digital's job—I'm here to put on a TV show." Digital's structure also left it at risk of being cut.

Being a "special project" at a time of cutbacks left it isolated and vulnerable.

By the time I moved from head of TV to the head of the entire organization, digital had matured. It made no sense to have digital operations as a separate division. People across all departments had to work in the new reality the digital world was creating. And so the first big structural change I made was making "digital" part of everyone's job.

Instead of having a separate silo, I integrated the members from the digital team into all departments. The digital sports expert went to the sports department, the news person in digital went to news, and so on. The content creators and producers would benefit from the expertise and skills the digital members brought and everyone would become cross-trained. No one could think of content being created for only one medium any longer. We were ushering in the age of "360 development" where multiple platforms became the natural way to go. It sounds so 101 now, but it was a hard sell. Some lamented the "disbanding of digital" when our goal was to reinforce the idea that digital wasn't one department's job, it was everyone's.

Any time you knock down a silo, people can see it as a loss for one, not a gain for the whole. Silos breed internal competition, and not usually the healthy kind, because the big picture can get lost in the territorial jockeying. And more often than not, the winner is the one who has the boss's ear. It was a typical hub-and-spoke scenario. In the situation I inherited at the CBC, I became the hub.

Each of the spokes represented a division overseen by a senior manager who was used to reporting back to the leader.

This meant the leader risked making decisions based on the isolated information stream from one spoke. It also could mean that decisions had less to do with surfacing the best data, but rather with which senior manager had the most influence with the boss. This happens in many traditional businesses. The most powerful silo was the one run by the manager with the most influence, the one who got in to see the boss last, the one with the loudest voice, or maybe even the one who golfed with the boss. I could see in an instant where valuable information could be lost and the quality of decisions threatened. And so, in the run-up to the Sochi Olympics, I decided it was prime time to try something completely different.

Silo-busting Is Woman's Work

WINNING BACK THE RIGHTS to broadcast the 2014 Olympics, after competitors had aired the two previous games, was a coup, and one of my proudest moments at the CBC. Much had changed in the broadcast universe since the CBC had shared the Beijing games with Canadians in 2008. Viewers didn't want to watch one sport on one channel at a particular time, with the broadcaster making all their viewing choices for them. They needed, and wanted, a multi-directional offering across television, radio, and the Internet, including mobile apps. Putting on a great show of multiple sports, on multiple platforms, from a distant time zone, would demand greater collaboration between departments than there had ever been before at the CBC.

Luckily, by then, digital expertise was well integrated across the network. Everyone who had a role to play in producing

Olympic coverage—sports, news, scheduling, revenue—now knew how to execute digitally. Yet the departments themselves were still a long way from integration. If I was going to pull off an event this big, on time and on a very limited budget, I needed the best of the best from experienced leaders and teams across the company. And I needed them to work together.

In my career I have always tried to focus on creating the best overall user experience. Now, we had to figure out how viewers across Canada could watch what they wanted, when and where they wanted, and still stay within our budget as we maximized revenue. Being efficient internally wouldn't be enough. I knew from the outset we'd need outside broadcast partners, because the public wanted more than the bandwidth the CBC could deliver on its own. The silos, inside and outside, had to come down.

More than a year before the games began, I pulled all the senior managers into a room together: experts in sports production, news, marketing, broadcast operations, revenue generation and more. I told them that they were all now a part of the team that would be planning the CBC's Olympic coverage, with the head of sports rights, Jeffrey Orridge, taking the lead as my delegate—the *chef de mission*. Because, I said, the coverage would only be as strong as their ability to cooperate. Our success would be measured by the enjoyment of Canadians watching their Olympic team compete. We were going to show Canadians the best Olympic experience they'd ever had: that was the vision. The goal was delivering that best experience on time and on budget, using all the technology and partnership benefits we could muster. Then I left them to it.

Jeffrey checked back in regularly, keeping me up to date on progress, on important staffing or technology decisions, asking my advice if the team had come to an impasse. To me, that's how we need to lead today: being there at the top to clearly express the aims, set goals and expectations, ensure people have what they need to work, and then get out of the way so they can get the job done.

In this case, the work had a lot to do with conversation. Brought into a room to find common ground, they had to talk; the more they talked, they more they learned from each other. Everyone soon started to see the big picture. It's no wonder that a recent study from the Center for Collective Intelligence at MIT found the intelligence score of a group rises when everyone gets equal airtime. When the production team, who wanted to present the highest and best quality coverage of the Games, found itself with production costs piling up and threatening the budget, it turned to the research and revenue team to find out how to prioritize its spending by sporting event. Which events connected to the most audience, and would feed the most revenue back to the plan? Sometimes the answers were surprising—not at all what anyone had assumed. Each team gained a new appreciation for the challenges facing the other. Scheduling faces the issue of building a smart lineup while balancing the volume of sports, the need for live coverage and the time difference in Russia. When that challenge is clearly explained, suddenly everyone understands the importance of sublicensing our broadcast rights to other broadcasters in order to get the programming out on as many signals and platforms as possible, which is what we did by sublicensing to Rogers and Bell. Not to mention the advantage of getting our brand and our talent exposed on those big private broadcasters.

Before long, the questions, the answers, and the sharing make everyone not just aware of, but truly appreciative of, the situation of others. Yes, they still championed their own expertise, but now they were all on the same team. And that created a profound connectedness on a human level. On that basis, trust and respect build. People recognize they cannot be expert in everything, but now they know who to call when they need help. That transparency results in efficiencies and helps to realize millions in savings that goes back into a budget for the whole team to share. When one wins we all win.

Collaboration, trust and communicating with co-workers: these areas should be considered part of any performance review. I soon added these soft skills as key performance indicators in executive senior staff reviews, stipulating that no one could overachieve and reap a bonus unless they passed that test. (Everyone plays differently when they have some skin in the game.) Where objective and key results describe company and individual goals in terms of numbers, pulling in a million viewers or a million dollars, those aren't the only important measures of success. How you contribute to the overall success of the team is equally important, lest the lone wolf who does anything to hit the target number leaves a path of destruction while trying to get to that goal. It's how you act as a whole person that should matter at work. Individual contributors need to see the value in helping along the rest of the team.

It's not always the easiest process to manage. Salespeople in particular hate this approach and who can blame them? They made their careers hitting targets. But in my experience they soon see the value in the exercise because hitting those numbers is a lot easier when you have a whole team of people to help do it. I left the CBC before Sochi went to air. But I knew it was in great shape and in the hands of a well-functioning team. CBC's remarkable, innovative coverage of the Sochi Olympics set a new standard in broadcasting the Games. True to the original vision, it marked the first time that despite limited resources, multiple sports were available across multiple platforms for Canadians to enjoy as they pleased: more than 1,500 record-breaking hours of it. Because we partnered with Rogers and Bell, which broadcast CBC's coverage on their many sports channels, we had the added benefit of selling commercial airtime on those platforms to fund our business model. And with steady live streaming, curated primetime content and a specialized mobile app, the coverage also attracted audiences and rave reviews from Europe and the US. It was an incredible achievement for the CBC at a time when another round of cuts had taken a huge toll on morale. And while I may have kicked off the effort by defining a vision for what Sochi could mean to CBC and its audience, it's the team who deserves total credit for implementing it. By the time Sochi was on the air, I was building another team—from scratch and silo-free—at Twitter.

One for All, and All for One

WITH A MANDATE TO BUILD the brand and grow the business, I made it a priority at the new Twitter office I launched in Toronto to create a team of advisers from across departments. Together, we strategized and decided the calendar of topics we'd tackle. I've come to see such equality as not just being good for business, and for women, but for seeding good morale from the ground up. People want to have a seat at the table, and not just to "be heard." They want to contribute and know that all the hours they spend at work are meaningful.

Much has been written about how much people hate their jobs. Surveys and studies have produced evidence that too many of us, men and women, find their workplaces soulless and disappointing. A large national study by Carleton University researchers in 2012 found that only 23 percent of working Canadians are highly satisfied with life. That was half as many as in 1991. A 2013 Gallup report found just 30 percent of employees in the US feel engaged at work, and the big picture is even worse: around the world, based on data from 142 countries, only 13 percent of employees feel engaged. I believe much of the dissatisfaction and disconnection stems from people feeling that they have little ownership over what they do. Whereas if each individual man and woman feels like he or she is a valued part of a team, free to step up with ideas and be heard by the boss as well as peers, it would go a long way to boosting job satisfaction. It would also set that individual on a course toward leadership.

After I discussed this idea in terms of women in the workplace at a recent talk I gave, a woman in her twenties approached me. She told me she'd found my talk intriguing but wondered how on earth it could be applied to her situation. "I'm not a boss," she said. "I'm not going to be a boss any time soon."

I understood her perspective perfectly. Not everyone has a job at the top, but everybody wants to make a meaningful contribution. When I asked her what she did at her company she told me she was a researcher. I asked her to describe her job in a little more detail and she explained that an important part of it was a daily meeting in which the sales guys asked her questions: she provided the answers that helped them do their job.

"When you are going through all that research you must see things that the salespeople don't ask about? Trends or points that would be of collective interest to the group, right?"

She agreed that she did.

I suggested that if that was the case she didn't need an invitation to share her insights. "Instead of waiting for the questions," I said, "what about going to the person who organizes the meetings and saying that you've noticed this point in your research and offer to put a brief presentation together for the next meeting, a few slides of information that could be helpful to the group? Doing that would put you in a position of leading, because you have this wealth of data, and you have taken the initiative to share it so the group can benefit." The woman said she hadn't thought of it that way, and promised me she'd give it a shot.

When I thought about it later, it struck me that, like that young woman, we all have opportunities to step up, to contribute and show initiative in the workplace. You don't have to be the boss to be a leader. You can lead an industry, a company, a division, or even a project of just one—you. When you seize those opportunities, you are leading. The more you act like a leader, the more you learn to be one. And the more you will be seen as one.

Like strengthening a muscle, it just takes practice.

So Long, Superwoman

I REMEMBER A POPULAR perfume commercial from the '80s that featured a seductive blonde singing about how she could bring home the bacon, fry it up in the pan and never let you forget you're a man—"'Cause," as she belted out in the big finish, "I'm a woman." As she sang, she danced through a rapid series of wardrobe changes, from business attire to casual clothes and then a slinky cocktail dress. The ad, for a fragrance called Enjoli, was such a hit the advertising agency created an extended version with the same woman crooning that she could also make it home at five o'clock and read the children *Tickety Tock*. (The ad still garners views on YouTube—more than 250,000 and counting.) It was less of a jingle than an absurd ode to the myth of the modern, multi-tasking female: able to leap corporate ladders in a single bound, cook faster than a speeding bullet, mother her children between meetings and still find the time (and energy) to remind her man, that yes, he *was* a man. The outfit that she should have been wearing was tights and a cape.

Most of the female executives I knew at the time already realized that the idea of being a superwoman was nonsense. When it came to life's great hat trick—love, kids and career— they felt that a woman could score two of these, but never three. If you wanted to bring home the bacon, and have a man, kids didn't fit easily into the picture. If you wanted kids and a career, keeping your man happy, or keeping him at all, seemed impossible. In the late 1980s, *Canadian Business* magazine ran a cover story on a group of women who were as close to achieving those coveted corner offices as any woman in Canada at the time: the interviews revealed that none of them thought they could have it all, and despite their excellence at work, most of them had fantasies of escaping the corporate world and devoting themselves to their children and husbands.

The divorce rate seemed to back them up. During the 1980s, it soared to historic highs in the western world. In Canada, it was projected that 50.6 percent of people who married in 1987 would divorce before they reached their thirtieth wedding anniversaries. The spike was due in part to the introduction of less onerous grounds for divorce, but the women's movement was also thought to play a role, which to a certain extent encouraged women to look after number one. The professionally successful women I knew were variously divorced with children, or childless and still married, or living child-free with long-time partners.

Of course, I took this all in, but I was sure, as each new generation tends to be, that things would be better for me. I couldn't imagine life without a family. Nor could I imagine myself without a career, and I had chosen a partner I believed supported the ambitions of a modern woman.

First, Do Not Judge Other Women

AT A VERY YOUNG AGE I married a man who had grown up with a mother who was a nurse, which meant he'd had his share of babysitters and pouring his own bowls of cereal. Together, we had agreed to put off having kids for a few years until I was earning enough to afford good child care. I assumed a new age of equality had dawned.

When I got pregnant with my first child, I was twenty-nine and president of Paragon International. Two weeks after my daughter was born, I was back on the job, though working from home. After six weeks, I was back in the office. By the time my baby was ten weeks old, I was on the other side of the Atlantic in Cannes, selling Paragon's shows to an international roster of broadcasters.

Many people were surprised at my approach to motherhood, perhaps even shocked, and they found ways to let me know it. My baby was home with her father, but also a full-time nanny. Still, people inquired after the well-being of my husband with awe, as though a father at home with a baby was a miracle. In interviews, journalists asked about the maternity leave I took or, rather, didn't take. *Only six weeks, when* [at the time] *Canadian women were entitled to six months?* In media profiles, they cast it as evidence of my drive and ambition. The reactions and the coverage had a distinctly judgemental undercurrent: How could you leave your baby? How could you put your career before your child?

Yet how it looked and how it was were two very different stories. We'd actually thought hard about how I could have enough time to be with my child in those early months. We had tried to time my pregnancy so I would deliver in the summer when things slowed down in the television industry and I could take the six months off. For a while, it looked like everything was going just as we had planned. Then my husband lost his job. Laid off from the museum where he worked as a carpenter, his severance pay ran out, ironically, the day I gave birth. Paragon didn't offer any paid maternity leave and I wasn't in a position that could influence changing such a policy. It was (and often still is) standard in the entertainment industry that additional support for leave is not a part of the employment package. Quite suddenly, I went from being our family's main breadwinner to its only breadwinner. Taking time off was a luxury we couldn't afford.

So, as many women do, I fought back the longing to be with my newborn, spread myself across sleepless nights and busy days. I also took my breast pump to work. At the office, the sound of the pump became as familiar as a ringing phone: *ahhwoogah . . . ahhwoogah . . .* When I went to Cannes, the pump came with me because I was determined to resume nursing my daughter when I got home. But in France, the higher voltage at the hotel revved my pump into hyper-drive—*ahhwoogah-ahhwoogah-ahhwoogah*—then, suddenly, it quit altogether. With no release, my swollen breasts turned to concrete. By the time I reached home, my milk had dried up. I was a mess of hormones and guilt, letting down the "breast is best" campaign and feeling a strike against me as a mother. Yes, I didn't miss tying myself into knots trying to pump on schedule while running a business. But I did feel desolate over losing the middle of the night and early morning feeds when my daughter and I felt like the only people in the universe, and I felt simply and completely essential to her. I realized that new dawn of equality was still a long way off.

Sure, women's horizons were broader than they had ever been, but we weren't so much liberated as we were prisoners of expectation: our own for ourselves, and those of a society still wed to 1950s values about the moral obligations of women.

Those early months of motherhood were among the most emotionally difficult periods in my life. They were made only more so by the judgements and assumptions of others. What right does anyone have to judge the most personal decisions in your life: If you have children, when to have your children, how much time you take away from work when they're born, how long you breastfeed, or how you and your family decide to raise your baby? No one knows the forces at play in someone's life. And no one has the right to judge. Whether we make personal decisions by necessity or by choice, they're personal. We have to grant one another the freedom to make our best decisions.

Yet we do judge, and women especially judge each other often, and often harshly. We are parked into camps of "stay-at-home" and "working" mothers when that's a completely false divide. Having babies and raising children is work, period. The choice a family makes in how each parent contributes to raising that child is a choice for that family alone. We are all just trying to make it work; what works best for one family will not be the same as for another. Different women will make different decisions, yet we are all women in this together. Not appreciating that we are all in it together is what lies at the root of those ridiculous "mommy wars" that the media fuels, even manufactures (nothing like pouncing on a *gurrl* fight to sell papers and use as clickbait).

In my opinion, these conflicts are a destructive attempt to divide and conquer women, and academia has played right into the battle. Researchers in many countries launched huge long-term studies to investigate the "effects" of working mothers on children, as if their offspring might be at high risk of growing up to be sociopaths; as if only a mother who works outside the home, not a father, might jeopardize a child's future; and, worst of all, as if the many women who need to work to keep their families afloat are doing their children a disservice. We need to shed the misperceptions about the impact on children of working mothers, but there are signs that we are ready to do that work. In the run-up to announcing a new initiative on gender issues, the Harvard Business School released a study of 50,000 adults in 25 countries that showed that children of working mothers, far from being damaged, reaped some advantages. As the May 15, 2015, column in the *New York Times*, Claire Cain Miller, a reporter for The Upshot, the paper's politics and policy venture, summed it up: "Daughters of working mothers completed more years of education, were more likely to be employed and in supervisory roles and earned higher incomes. Having a working mother didn't influence the careers of sons, which researchers said was unsurprising because men were generally expected to work—but sons of working mothers did spend more time on child care and housework."

Despite such research, when it comes to explaining the dearth of women in leadership roles, having children is still cast as the mother of all issues.

Blame the Cape

WHEN BERKELEY SOCIOLOGIST Arlie Hochschild explored the lives of mothers who work outside the home in her landmark book, *The Second Shift,* published in 1989, she estimated the amount of daily housework and child care women were doing outside of their paying jobs totalled an extra month of work per year compared to their spouses' workload. What's remarkable is that despite all the judging I just mentioned, and the double duty women assumed when they started also working outside the home, our progress in the workplace has been as impressive as it has been. But we all know it's hard, and that's why, of all the questions I'm asked about my career trajectory, at the top of the list is "How do you do it?" as not only a woman, but a woman with children. Women with demanding jobs who also have children tend to be seen as fiercely driven (if not slightly demented) females who want to "have it all."

I blame the cape. The media portrayal of the modern female as superwoman has stuck. It's the standard to which women are still held, and that's been superdestructive.

History has a lot to do with why it is such a sticky idea. Once upon a time, girls were groomed to be perfect daughters, wives and mothers. Now, of course, female territory has expanded outside these roles, but so has that quest for perfection. We want to be straight-A students, professionally successful, excellent and attentive mothers caring for our families in beautiful homes, as we exercise our taut bodies, foster our happy marriages and always have something organic baking in the oven. Women tend to view anything less than perfect as a failure, usually their own.

I have twisted myself into a pretzel trying to prove (to whom, might be the question) that I am both a consummate professional and a devoted parent. On another trip to Cannes, in between closing million-dollar distribution deals, I spent the flight hours there and back furiously knitting a full-body bear costume so my daughter would have it in time to wear for her first Halloween. She was four months old. The only person demanding that she have the best handmade costume ever was me!

Fuelled by media portrayals that perpetuate society's expectations of what the successful modern female is supposed to be, we set ludicrous standards for ourselves in all areas of our lives. The quest for perfection starts early. A 2007 article in *The Nation* dubbed it "The Supergirl Syndrome": "At the top of her class, kicks ass on the soccer field and the debate team, plays a mean violin and is the life of every party. Everyone loves her: mom, dad, the coach, teachers, the boys at school and, of course, the media. The supergirl is the embodiment of the 'go-girl' feminism that has become the staple of mainstream coverage, the focus of feel-good stories about female empowerment. Everything a boy can do, this gal can do and more . . . and maybe even better." It's no wonder women enter the workforce with lower levels of self-confidence, lower expectations of what they might achieve professionally and why that insidious Imposter Syndrome—the self-destructive sense that you are a fraud unworthy of your position, just a breath away from being "found out"—is likened to an epidemic among high-achieving women.

By the late '90s, many women gave up on trying to make their way in the workplace at the same time as leading the way on the home front. They were fed up trying to have, be, or do it all. Kids came along and suddenly life's vaunted hat trick seemed as elusive as it had to the women execs I'd known in the 1980s. A study from the Pew Research Center found that the proportion of mothers not working outside the home rose in the US to 29 percent in 2012, up from 23 percent in 1999—a reversal of the long-term decline of "stay-at-home" mothers in the last three decades of the twentieth century.

In 2003, *The New York Times Magazine* documented the trend of well-educated, professional women cutting back in order to work part-time or quitting altogether as proof that the feminist movement had stalled. It described these women as being part of "the opt-out revolution" and included Harvard Business School stats that revealed that only 38 percent of its female graduates in the classes of 1981, 1985 and 1991 were working full-time. Meanwhile, the US Census showed that the number of new mothers going back to work was falling and the number of women staying home to care for their children had increased by 13 percent in less than a decade. (Interestingly, the same trend did not surface in Canada, where the number of women who stay home to raise children has steadily declined. This may have something to do with the fact that Canadian maternity leave jumped from seventeen weeks to a full year during this time period. Even so, 2009 data from Statistics Canada shows women without children are much more likely to be employed than those who have kids.)

The women in the *Times* article were generally affluent. They had high-earning partners whose incomes allowed them the luxury of choosing whether they wanted to work outside the home. But they were also the very well-educated, ambitious women who were expected to blaze the equality trail into the future, something they had once expected of themselves. Instead, they gave up trail-blazing to be with their children and find greater domestic harmony, maybe sure that their change in direction was temporary. (A follow-up feature a decade later found that while these women had no regrets about dropping out to raise their kids, opting out of the career track had been no guarantee of a happy marriage, and in some cases had put their financial independence and self-confidence in jeopardy. And opting back in was no simple matter.)

I remember reading the original article with a deep personal interest. I was heading up the specialty channels at Alliance Atlantis at the time; I had two daughters under the age of six and I was under a mountain of pressure. Any relationship can suffer when both parents work full-time. But in our marriage, my career became a source of bitterness. My daughters' father had gone back to school to become a teacher after being laid off, and I had supported him as I worked my way up through television's executive ranks and had a second baby. Yet the higher I rose, and the more money I made, the worse our relationship became. As he worked on reinventing his career, I had sped ahead, skewing the traditional lines of husband/wife, father/mother with my larger salary and big job.

Yet despite the steady demands of my job, I was often expected to be the go-to parent. My job was seen as being "just meetings," as opposed to the on-duty work life of a teacher. I was the one considered to have the more flexible schedule, so I often stayed home when the kids were sick, taking conference calls while I held back my daughter's hair as she threw up. Eventually our relationship broke down, and we broke up, as sociologists might have predicted.

A 2013 Pew study revealed that marriages in which a wife outearns her husband tend to be unhappy ones with higher rates of divorce. And that same year, researchers from the University of Chicago's Booth School of Business found that marriages in which the wife made more than her husband were actually relatively rare, either because the marriages didn't last or because women on course to outearn their spouses tended to reduce the number of hours they worked. Interestingly, when a wife's income did rise beyond her husband's, so did the amount of time she spent on household chores. Researchers suggested this may be guilt at work: high-earning women putting in extra time on the domestic front to please their partners or assuage that guilt is still prevalent among women who work.

We had it much easier than most working parents because I could afford a nanny. But it wasn't motherhood that made my work-life juggle miserable. Spending time with my girls was a gift. If it meant I had to catch the red-eye across the country to be back in time to join my daughter's class trip to the pumpkin patch, I'd do it (although I did stand, jet-lagged, amid those chattering toddlers, at risk of doing a face plant in that muddy field). Having kids is not incompatible with having a career. But it is vital that both partners are committed to doing what it takes to survive as a family.

In November 2014, the Harvard Business School released a persuasive study on that point. Based on interviews with

25,000 male and female HBS graduates, researchers concluded that children don't hold women back, their husbands do. Many women in the study reported that they were not meeting the career goals they had set for themselves in their twenties. This wasn't the result of choosing to opt out of the career track after they had children, but because they allowed their partners' careers to take precedence over their own; if they had to leave their job, often they did so reluctantly. In part because respondents said their employers had put them on "the mommy track" in subtle or overt ways. But also because their partners had too. More than half of Boomer and Gen X men said they expected their careers would take precedence over their partners'; while only 3 percent of Boomer women, and 7 percent of Gen X women, said their careers would come first.

Looking back, I don't think I truly understood what my ex-husband expected. We never had an in-depth conversation about the future before we married when I was just months out of university. I made assumptions, likely unfairly, about his attitudes because of his parents: his mother had the more steady job and pay. We never talked specifically about my ambitions and how we would reconcile them with the home life he wanted; nor did we discuss his goals or my visions of the family home. I assumed it was enough to know that he generally supported my hopes to build a successful career and arrange for good child care. Which is just further proof that assumptions are dangerous. Having a marriage that goes bad teaches some very tough lessons, but for me, the upside was that my failed marriage helped me figure out how to forge a good one.

In 2011, I married Zaib Shaikh. We'd met at the CBC when I was head of English language television and he was starring in *Little Mosque on The Prairie*. We weren't the first couple to meet at work, and I knew the protocol; when we started dating, I recused myself from decisions involving his work at the CBC. Also, unlike my first time around, long before we exchanged vows, we talked at length about how we'd structure our home life as two busy professionals and, more importantly, we agreed on how we'd try to do it.

It takes a brave man to take on everything I now brought to a relationship. I wasn't a fresh university grad. I had a big job, with big demands that spill outside office hours, regular travel cross-country, and now out-of-country. And two kids, whose custody I shared with my ex (ironically, divorce had managed to create a more even split in our parenting duties). One time early in our relationship, Zaib was out with another actor friend who asked if he was truly ready to "take it on." Not just the kids and the work, but the idea that when we walked into a room together, there would be certain times when he wasn't going to be the centre of attention—that would be me. Zaib insisted he was ready. He is a brave man.

And I knew that Zaib—an actor, director and producer with jobs that have taken him to the far corners of the globe; and, more recently, his role as Toronto's first film and entertainment commissioner—has a schedule as erratic as my own. But we are a team. We make decisions together, whether it's about what to order for dinner (and we order in *a lot*), or whether I should leave the CBC for Twitter, or whether he should become the city's film commissioner. And when it comes to sharing parenting responsibilities, I may be the preferred PB&J-maker on Saturday after tennis lessons, but Zaib is king of the paratha lunch and a valued wardrobe consultant. When my eldest went shopping to buy a prom outfit for her boyfriend, she sent Zaib pictures so he could advise on the tie she picked out. They have their own relationship and I couldn't describe what it is exactly, but it is exactly what it should be.

Today, I'd tell any woman considering marriage, my own daughters included, that they need to discuss how they want their future homes and families to operate, and that the discussion needs to be detailed and explicit. I'm convinced that the item that has been sorely missing from the have-it-all debate and the narratives of working mothers is men, and their expectations of their partners, career ambitions and visions for raising the next generation. For women, not spending enough time with their children is a source of guilt; for men, some are realizing that they miss out on something special, too, when they let themselves be chained to a desk and career. Last year, for example, when Mohamed El-Erian gave up his $100 million annual paycheque as CEO of the Pacific Investment Management Company, shocking the financial world, he said his decision was triggered by a note his ten-year-old daughter had written to him. It was a list of the significant events he had missed in her life because of work, including her first day of school, a parent-teacher meeting and her first soccer match.

While it appears that a few more men are walking away from jobs at the top of their careers to build better relationships with their kids (and to be clear, these are men who can *well afford* to walk away), society has a lot of catching up to do. Unfortunately, too often men who do stay home to raise their children are either stigmatized or, perversely, held up as a unicorn (look, he actually stayed home with a sick child or baked cupcakes for the class party: amazing!). The idea that women should hold up the home front is still so entrenched that many male executives, according to another recent Harvard paper, still think of "work–life balance" as a "women's issue." And why wouldn't they? Men are almost never asked how they "do it all," how they made it to the corner office, or to the Supreme Court, or to outer space. We know the answer. What has to change is the question. It's not "How do *you* do it all," but "How will *we* do it all."

This was a point made beautifully by Max Schireson. The CEO of MongoDB, a billion-dollar database company he'd helped to grow, resigned just seven months after El-Erian quit and for similar reasons: he said the travel demands of his job were robbing him of time he wanted to spend with his wife and three children. As Schireson described it in a blog post that went viral: "Earlier this summer, Matt Lauer [host of *The Today Show*] asked Mary Barra, the CEO of GM, whether she could balance the demands of being a mom and being a CEO. *The Atlantic* asked similar questions of PepsiCo's female CEO, Indra Nooyi. As a male CEO, I have been asked what kind of car I drive and what type of music I like, but never how I balance the demands of being both a dad and a CEO. . . . Friends and colleagues often ask my wife [a doctor and professor at Stanford University] how she balances her job and motherhood. Somehow, the same people don't ask me."

The press celebrated Schireson's resignation. "When a top CEO quits to be a better dad it's a giant leap forward for women execs," said the headline in *Fortune* magazine. And on Twitter, many comments were reminiscent of those "Ooh, you baked cookies" coos. People called it "brave . . . bold . . . honest." As one woman summed it up: "Best. Statement. Ever." I couldn't help but contrast the public reaction when a woman with a top job steps down to spend more time with her family. For one thing, she rarely makes news. Women sacrifice professional advancement and potential earnings to take care of their families day in and day out, and always have. In 2000, I made the hard decision to turn down an exciting television job offer in Manhattan because it would have been too difficult for my former husband to find work there, and too difficult for me to spend time with my girls. (I took the Hallmark job in Denver instead.) When a woman's decision to leave a high-profile job does become public, as it did when foreign policy expert Anne-Marie Slaughter left her director's job in Hillary Clinton's State Department to be closer to her two teenage sons, the fallout became rich fodder for the eternal can't-have-it-all debate. (Slaughter's 2012 article in *The Atlantic*, "Why Women Still Can't Have It All," quickly went viral, with over a million downloads in its first week.)

I've always thought the phrase itself was terribly imprecise. Exactly what is "it"? I would argue that whether you succeed or not depends entirely on what "it" means to you. Maybe "it" is having satisfying work that rarely places demands on you outside of nine-to-five, Monday-to-Friday hours, leaving your nights and weekends with your family undisturbed. Perhaps "it" is working part-time so you can pursue dreams of starting your own business while you raise your children. Or maybe "it" is becoming head of a multi-million-dollar corporation and having a family of five; in which case, you factor in the squadron of child care and domestic help you will need (and hopefully be able to afford) to keep your version of "it" from sabotaging your mental health.

The upshot is that "it" is up to an individual to define. And, let's face it, for the vast majority of working mothers, work is work: it's to pay the bills, and quitting is not an option. The same goes for many working fathers: they don't have the luxury of pondering the question. I've been there, counting subway tokens and statutory holidays to ensure I'd have enough to get me to the end of a month. I think the Rolling Stones essentially had it right: You can't always get what you want, but if you try, you might find you get what you need.

What's giving me hope now is that the world is in transition, and we are not alone. The work-life juggle isn't a woman's issue, it's a family issue—no matter the makeup of that family. No player scores a hat trick alone; it has to be a team effort. And this is the moment where if we move forward, we move forward together.

He for She, and Vice Versa

FINDING A HAPPY RHYTHM between work and home can no longer be called a woman's issue because it simply isn't one. Traditional gender identities are converging, with more women in the workplace (70 percent of women in North America) and men more involved in the home. As technology and demographic shifts remake the economy, and the culture, the workplace can no longer function as a rigid "man's world" and home is no longer the place where men can play "Mr. Mom."

There's been a tendency to analyze the evolution of the women's movement as a phenomenon unto itself: blossoming like an exuberant kid in the 1960s and '70s, shooting up with the growing pains of a moody teen through the '80s and '90s, and now maturing, becoming part of the wider social revolution under way, which includes a fledgling movement among men.

After all, the very nature of what constitutes family is shifting profoundly, not just the gender roles within it. We're experiencing the rise of single-parent homes; the recreation of the extended family as grandparents age or as children need longer to launch; gay and lesbian couples having children, people choosing not to have children, to name just a few. People are marrying later in their lives and having children later, if they are having them at all. You can't have a true social revolution with only half the population participating any more than you can exclude half the population from the professional talent pool. Women's roles and aspirations have been changing for a century, and, at last, albeit slowly, so are those of men.

Early signs of that change were evident to me about eighteen months after I opened the offices of Twitter Canada, during which time our staff grew from zero to thirty. It was September 2014, just after Labour Day weekend, and kids were heading back to school. Several employees called to let me know they'd be late, or away that whole morning, as they took their children in for the first day. At some point, it struck me that I'd heard from as many men as women. It was a nice revelation: a small sign of equality on the home front. Not only did employees have the freedom to take the morning to deliver their kids to school, but the duty had apparently been taken up by fathers as well as mothers. There have been other signs. During the time I was in charge at Twitter Canada the only employee to take a parental leave was a man, our head of research, who took paid leave to be off with his newborn daughter.

I was recently part of a panel of women in finance where we discovered we were living examples of the gender roles in transition. The eldest of us was married and chose to be childless: "There was just no way for us back then if we wanted a career." The second eldest had children, but was the breadwinner whose husband was able to move where her jobs took her. The youngest was a newly married woman confident that when it came time to start a family, she and her husband would work out raising the baby together, confident that technology, the nature of her job and her partner's commitment, would make the work-life juggle much easier for her than it had been for any of us who had gone before. And I don't doubt it.

There's a raft of evidence about the expanding domestic roles of men to bolster my front-line anecdotes. A 2014 Pew Center study found the number of stay-at-home dads has more than doubled in the last twenty-five years. Men are still firmly in the minority of parents who stay home, and many are home because of a disability or unemployment. But the segment of fathers who said they were choosing to be at home specifically to look after their children has expanded dramatically: it's jumped to 21 percent from 5 percent in 1989.

In part, the trend reflects new economic realities that have been especially tough on men. With the rapid shift from brawn to brain, from a manufacturing to a knowledge-based economy, many of the jobs traditionally held by males have disappeared. According to the US Bureau of Labor Statistics, during the recent recession, women lost just one job for every 2.6 jobs lost by men. Statistics Canada figures show that between 2008 to 2009, employment among men 25 and under declined nearly 10.8 percent, while for women in the same age group it fell by only 6.5 percent.

Women, meanwhile, now account for about 60 percent of university graduates, they're far more likely than men to graduate from the programs they start and in many fields they're earning more advanced degrees than men are. These achievements in learning are, bit by bit, translating into earnings. A woman is now the primary breadwinner in 40 percent of American households with children under 18, according to Pew Center research. That's compared to 11 percent in 1960. In Canada, the story is similar: households with women at the economic helm have nearly quadrupled, from 8 percent in 1976 to more than 31 percent in 2010. And interestingly, this StatsCan data shows the rise of female breadwinners is happening equally across the country, and across age groups. (Though education makes a significant difference: the higher the level, the more likely a woman is to be a female breadwinner.)

The increase is due, in part, to the rise of single mothers. But simple economics helps to explain it too; more couples are opting to have the higher-earning parent keep earning while the other parent becomes the main caregiver and manager of the household. And more and more, that higher earner is the woman, the wife, the mother. StatsCan data shows that between 1976 and 2010, the median annual income of men with full-time jobs hardly budged, while it jumped by more than 25 percent for women, who are more likely to hold jobs requiring cognitive versus manual skills. Women still earn a whole lot less than men overall, but this is an area where the gap is closing and having a real impact on the home front. In 2013, for instance, the *New York Times* reported that the number of women in finance with stay-at-home husbands has increased tenfold since 1980. The National At-Home Dad Network, started in 2003 by three fathers in the Washington,

DC, area, has grown into a national, even international, organization with seventy chapters across the US and Canada. And
demographic changes are contributing to the trend big time.

Many studies have found that Millennials believe that
professional goals should take a backseat to family responsibilities and personal aspirations. And the young men among
them are more likely than any males who have come before
them to have grown up with a working mother, or a single
mother, which may have given them a fresh perspective on
modern fatherhood. The Boston College Center for Work
and Family, for example, found Millennial and Gen X dads
took more time off to care for children than Baby Boomers
did. Its 2014 report, entitled *The New Dad*, based on surveys
and interviews with nearly three thousand fathers, found
more than three out of four dads expressed the desire to
spend more time with their kids. More than two out of three
said they and their partners should evenly split caring for
their children, and slightly more than half said they would
seriously consider staying home to be full-time dads.

I don't for a moment think this transition will happen
overnight (generational change never does), nor that it will be
universal or painless. A profound disconnect—and reckoning—
already lies on the horizon. Those same fathers in the Boston
study who are keen to spend time with their kids and equally
share parenting, also report that they're looking for jobs with
greater responsibility; while two out of three felt parenting
responsibilities should be 50/50, less than one out of three
said it actually is. I'd say fathers of the twenty-first century—
and the sons they raise—will face their own pressures to be
superdads. But their desire to be more involved in raising

their children will also add to the pressure companies are facing to accommodate the *whole* lives of the people who work for them.

Eggs and Leaves

ANYTIME A TOP male or female executive resigns to spend more time with family, the same question surfaces: Are high-powered, high-demand jobs incompatible with parenthood—not motherhood or fatherhood, but parenthood? Our social challenge isn't just to find ways, as employees, to cope with the responsibilities of home and work, but also for companies to figure out how to help their employees cope. And it's not about companies just trying to be "nice" to their workers. The job market is global and fiercely competitive, so it's in the interest of business to recruit and retain talent.

It just so happens that in today's world, increasingly, that talent is female. With so much evidence that women drive higher performance, the work world has a whole lot of catching up to do to overcome gender imbalance—particularly in its highest ranks.

A concerted effort is now under way by a staggering and eclectic mix of industries eager to bring more women into their fold: the life sciences, energy, finance, law—basically, most every field from tech to trucking (yes, trucking). The catch is that females are far more likely than males to leave their jobs for their families. So figuring out ways to keep female employees on staff, and support their climb up the ladder, has become as important to companies as recruiting women in the first place. The imperative to attract and keep their women is forcing employers to get ever more creative in building a culture with policies to help women succeed: flexible schedules, generous leaves, on-site child care and mentoring programs. The tech industry, for instance, where the lack of women has been a particularly hot topic, has taken some unprecedented, and unorthodox, steps. For instance, both Apple and Facebook are reportedly paying to freeze the eggs of their female employees.

The biological clock has always been a barrier to the boardroom for a woman, ticking down to its final life-giving moments just as she hits her career stride. (Never mind the urgency to find the right partner before her eggs hit their best-before date.) And while society has lagged behind the shifting realities of gender roles, science has not. Just as the birth control pill allowed women to separate sex from reproduction, the burgeoning field of reproductive technologies may give women the chance to separate age from procreation. It could allow a woman the freedom to have kids, and a career, on her own terms and her own schedule. The procedure involves extracting and freezing a woman's eggs when she's in her twenties or thirties. If all goes well, they can be thawed and are still viable at a later date.

The tech giants have described it as policy designed to empower women to do their best work without biology compromising their efforts. But of course the move set off a storm of controversy, a "mommy-to-be war." Some people were horrified that an employer would suggest women delay motherhood to focus on their work, the implication being that it pressures women to choose work over starting a family. Others applauded the move. Online and in the press, a number of women wrote commentaries about how egg freezing was finally a chance at a level playing field.

I tend to side with those who see the egg-freezing benefit as a positive development, a valuable perk for any woman who wants to take advantage of it. And that's the crucial point. When, and how, to have children is a personal decision, and, again, it's one for a woman to make for herself and not be judged for what she decides.

New reproductive technologies are always controversial. When IVF debuted, people were aghast, too, and skeptical that it would ever take off as a mainstream baby-making method. Yet today, about 1 percent of newborns in North America had their start in a "test tube" and many Fortune 500 companies cover IVF as an employee health benefit. I suspect the story could be similar with egg freezing (a number of other companies, including Google, are also reported to be considering offering it).

But what does irk me about the egg-freezing policy is the old-fashioned message it still sends about the obligations of women. Why should only women receive such an incentive to defer motherhood? Why isn't there a similar carrot for men, a policy that says, "Hey guys, here's what we'll do for you if you delay becoming a father while you're concentrating on developing professionally?" There isn't one because the view persists that fatherhood takes no toll on a man's ability to do his work, because he won't have to miss days to care for his kid, or come to work exhausted because of sleepless nights with a baby. It's assumed that professionally he can still plow onward and upward after he becomes a parent because parenting is primarily the mother's job, not his.

Happily, there are signals that change is afoot here too. More companies (and countries) are offering male employees paid parental leaves, as they do women. The new father at Twitter Canada who took a paternal leave was entitled to three months paid. Several major tech companies, including Google, Facebook, Yahoo and Reddit, all provide fathers with paid paternity leaves that range from seven to seventeen weeks. By country, leaves for fathers vary widely, with the US having one of the worst (including its maternity leaves for women) and Canada having one of the best. Unfortunately, men who take advantage of parental leaves report that they face the same career penalties that women do, but also have to confront an ugly social backlash, as if only wimps would want to do such a thing. But the only way that attitude is going to change is if men stick to it. The more fathers who take parental leaves, the more involved in parenting they will be from the get-go. Slowly, society, and the workplace, will accept it as a universal necessity. Over time, employers will come to appreciate the wisdom of extending leaves, benefits and flex schedules to all employees, regardless of gender. Then everybody wins. Men have the chance to be more involved with their children and women are free, if they choose, to stay more involved in work. From my perspective, that's critical; what you do at work in those early years could set the stage for how smoothly the long-term juggle of work and family will play out for you.

The Myth of Work–Life Balance

IN *LEAN IN*, SHERYL SANDBERG beseeches women not to let the prospect of having a family derail career plans or shape professional choices. Sandberg, Facebook's chief operating officer, argues that if women try harder, show more gumption and live their work, more women will rise to the top and the ambition gap will be filled. Her perspective makes an important contribution to the conversation around the challenges of women and work. But to my mind it also seems out of step in offering the well-meaning advice that for a woman to be as successful as a man, she should act like one.

Sandberg makes a case that, essentially, women are not reaching professional heights because we don't really know how to try. Her focus is mostly on what women are not doing, or not doing well: negotiating, tooting their own horns and so on. There's a lot of truth to what she says, but I think it's better to focus on what women do right and how what we bring to the table is crucial for corporate success moving forward. This past May, as I was finishing this book, Sandberg's forty-seven-year-old husband and the father of their two children, David Goldberg, CEO of SurveyMonkey—a man she described in her book as a true partner, her best friend and love of her life—died in a tragic accident during a family vacation in Mexico. It was a brutal reminder of the fragility of life and of what truly matters. In moments like these, it feels like what matters most is creating the life that fits each of us best—whatever our backgrounds, ambitions or definitions of success—so that we live every day without regret.

Isn't it true that our ultimate, seemingly elusive goal as women, and men, is to find fulfilling ways to work that still allow room for pleasure, personal happiness and loving relationships? Succeeding shouldn't mean having to work ever harder just for the sake of "getting ahead." Many of us have no need to scale the heights of the corporate world to feel successful; definitions of a life well lived are personal.

That said, there are definitely times in a career when putting your shoulder into it is critical—yes, as in *leaning in.* And as women, we need to keep our heads up enough to recognize when those important times appear. Taking the right chances to distinguish yourself, show initiative and make a contribution can happen anywhere along a career path. Those opportunities don't always lead instantly to a promotion or a raise. But they become moments that matter and pay important dividends down the line; every time a woman establishes herself as a leader, she builds important professional and personal capital. Eventually that capital translates into professional flexibility, giving you greater control over how, and even when, you work.

I don't always juggle my work, business travel and home life with the deftness people assume I must, given my responsibilities and accomplishments. Balls do get dropped. I forget to check the kids' homework. I'm forced to reschedule a meeting because I took on too much in one day. The saving grace is that my position affords me the luxury of flexibility. I am not watching the clock on a double shift, worried that I am going to be fifteen minutes late for the daycare pick-up time and not only collect a tired and hungry toddler but be charged $35 extra. For many parents, and especially women, that is working life. And I'm in awe of every day people in such situations who keep pulling it off.

As Anne-Marie Slaughter noted in her *Atlantic* feature, the ability to have a flexible work schedule depends largely on the career path you choose. In my own case, I never could have been that go-to parent when my daughters were young if I had not first invested several years of effort into building my career. I wouldn't have had the same freedom if I was still working as an assisstant. I am grateful every day for the flexibility a job like mine allows. It's why I advise younger women to take stock of why they are afraid of taking the next career step. What looks like a more demanding job may bring with it the flexibility a lower-level job doesn't allow, and in some ways life may become a little easier.

Like it or not, the work world is still, and will always be, a results-driven realm. Maybe that's where the saying "work hard, play hard" comes from. My performance gave me the freedom to stay home when I needed to, or spend a blurry-eyed morning in the pumpkin patch. The good news is that with companies hungrier than ever for a skill set women can bring to the table, the more opportunities there are for women to show how they can lead and earn the power to work, play and live by their own rules.

And this is important, because along with the elusive "have-it-all" brass ring we've been primed to capture, the other concept that does a disservice to parents everywhere is the idea that you should strive for work–life balance. You may as well hunt unicorns. The very word "balance" suggests that somehow you can give equal importance and time to all corners of your life at the same time. The person who loses most in that equation is you; if exhaustion doesn't get to you, the guilt will.

The idea of balance doesn't reflect how the world works, or how we truly spend our time. It's not about achieving balance, it's about flow. We swing from one priority to the next, pushing hard at work and then pulling back to be with family. How hard you push and pull depends entirely on the moment. There are high-pressure times on the job when deadlines loom, trips need to be taken, or tough decisions have to be made, and you work flat out for a long stretch without making it home for dinner. But there are other times when a sick child or parent or spouse, say, or simply a much-needed vacation, takes precedence over any job. The key is to aim for a career in which you can earn the freedom to achieve work–life flow.

In the next chapter, I'll explore how technology is not just changing the way business works, but profoundly altering the way people work. It's allowing women, and men, to manage the conflicting demands of career and family in ways that were never before possible, allowing us to multi-task, virtually be many places at once and change roles in a click.

Now we ditch that superhero cape for a really good smartphone.

[VII]

No Walls and
No Corner Offices

IN TALKS I GIVE ON THE new opportunities for women in leadership, I often include a reminder of the old guy in the corner office: a slide of the evil Mr. Burns from *The Simpsons*. The sight of Homer's boss—obsessed with inflating his own power and forever forgetful of his employees' names—never fails to spark a roomful of laughter. It's not just that the old stereotypes of corporate leadership Mr. Burns represents are passé, they are *so* passé, they're a joke.

Not that long ago, leading by decree was the norm. In the golden age of industrialization, there was a big boss on high and an army of general managers to do his bidding. And it was *his* bidding, as it was a golden age of patriarchy too. Each employee had a defined role with specific tasks, all of which were assigned and assessed by his manager. Employees showed up to the same place at the same time, and the pattern of a working day was more predictable than the weather. What customers knew about your product or service was basically what you chose to tell them. It was the heyday of hierarchy represented by a primitive command-and-control culture probably best summed up by an infamous complaint from the legendary Henry Ford: "Why is it that every time I ask for a pair of hands, they come with a brain attached?"

Managing became a little more complicated through the second half of the twentieth century. Competition went global, markets were deregulated, and along came new industries, companies and some seventy million Baby Boomers. According to a 2002 article, "Understanding the four generations to enhance workplace management," published in the *AFP Exchange*, a magazine for global finance executives, Boomers brought their own spitfire culture to the workplace: "On the job, Boomers arrive early and leave late, visibility is key. The longer the day, the higher the pay . . ." That generational shift in attitude added spokes to the centralized hub of the former leadership model, bringing the rise of the C-suite that has blossomed ever since. Corner offices expanded to become corridors of power, with a specialized chief who reported to the CEO, manning every division: CFOs and COOs, CIOs and CMOs and so on. And yes, it's mostly been men doing the manning.

The point is that for more than a century, all variations on the management model have been hierarchical, whether the hierarchy was centralized or spread out among the C-suite. But the information age has changed almost everything about the way we work—the where, the when, and, most significantly, the how—and as a result the top-down model makes no sense. Our customers have become our bosses and we need to manage "out," not down.

Small-Town World

TECHNOLOGY HAS BEEN THE great leveller. It's reshaped the world in ways that are profoundly different from the past. The last thirty years alone have brought us personal computers, email, tablets, smartphones, cloud computing, Wi-Fi and social networking. More than three billion people are active online. Nearly two billion, or close to a quarter of the world's population, uses social media, and, according to a 2015 report compiled by the global marketing firm We Are Social, there are now more active mobile connections than there are people on the planet. Call it disruptive, or transformative, but tech really has turned the world into a global village; everyone is connected to someone and someone else's business, and news, truth and gossip travel at small-town speeds. And like a village, rightly or wrongly, the online court of public opinion metes out its own brand of justice, swift and sometimes merciless.

What companies, corporations, and, to some extent, even countries have lost in this global village is the ability to control the agenda. The power of institutions and organizations to direct people's behaviour has been eroded, and with it the ability of any leader to arbitrarily call the shots. Power has shifted. When governments want to exert control over their citizens, they fight the public's access to social media. When companies want to reach consumers, they turn to the net. When consumers want to consume they do their due diligence online. With individual voices that can be heard far and wide, the information age has brought a new transparency to society. It's made every organization beholden to the individual customer as a new kind of stakeholder and forced the flattening of hierarchies. It's put real power in the hands of people.

Through the net and social media, everyday people, regardless of status or station, have an unrivalled ability to inform and be informed, to praise and to punish. It's a power that drives customer reviews, boycotts, protests, revolutions and web uprisings that can blow up in an instant. It's the kind of power that can prompt Nestlé to find a sustainable source of palm oil and stop the deforestation in Indonesia by Sinar Mas. It can cost United Airlines 10 percent of its share price—a whopping $180 million hit—for refusing to compensate a Canadian musician for breaking his guitar. It can push Coca-Cola and PepsiCo to drop a controversial ingredient from their beverages, convince the Bank of America to abandon an unpopular debit-card fee and enable a class of fourth graders to persuade Universal Studios to add an environmental message to its promotion of *The Lorax*. Social media have prompted a modern-day recasting of David and Goliath, in which ordinary people—even children—can make titans buckle.

It's no surprise that businesses feel vulnerable and exposed. Old business models and leadership structures are broken. Even basic principles of how to run a company have changed and so must our thinking about what it takes to succeed in business. While it might be tempting to focus on nothing but the minefields ahead, what I see from the frontier of these changing times is a landscape of tremendous opportunity for those who are willing to listen, to learn and adapt. And that translates into golden opportunities for women especially, for whom listening, learning and adapting have always been among our strong suits. It won't be easy.

Mistakes will be made, and uncertainty will be a devoted companion. But if you are keen to collaborate and form new kinds of partnerships with the people you work *with* and *for*, the future is yours.

We've Come a Long Way from Mr. Burns, Baby

THERE WERE NO RULE BOOKS for me to follow when I started Twitter Canada. The playbook was ours to create. In the first year, "ours" meant me, a smartphone, and six staff who didn't yet know each other. We were all in it together, starting something brand new in a country that hadn't yet done much business with Twitter. We didn't have precedents to fall back on, so when one of us learned something, we shared it with the others: *"Who has a presentation I can use with a bank?" "Here you go." "Anyone have the information on how Twitter appeals to moms?" "I saw it here: let me flip it to you."* We occupied an open office space, literally and figuratively without walls, and we built the business on a strategy that every team member helped to create.

The beauty of Twitter is that it is a platform for expression, and open conversation. As I figured out how to build a team that could help our clients overcome the challenges of operating in a world gone digital, we abided by the principles of listening and discussing. We were able to build the Canadian office quickly by creating a safe place for our partners in a digital environment that can feel like the Wild West, where we and our clients could try new initiatives, and sometimes fail, but always learn something important about this curious new world.

From my experience in television, I'd already seen how valuable social media could be in connecting a corporation to its customers, or, in my case, viewers and listeners. The web provided an unparalleled and precious chance to gauge audience reaction and understand viewers better. Instead of having to rely solely on focus group feedback, or wait for nightly ratings report cards that estimated how many people watched a show without the context of why they watched or how they felt about what they saw, Twitter suddenly gave me a glimpse into the real-time opinions of viewers. It was like eavesdropping: on Twitter I could listen in on those street-corner conversations I knew were so important. Some of what I "overheard" informed key programming decisions I made. Fan reaction over the cancellation of the *Murdoch Mysteries* TV series on Citytv, for example, was a major tipoff to make a deal with its producers to revive the show on CBC (it's still going strong).

The possibilities for business to benefit from what it sees and hears online are limitless. All sorts of companies and executives now turn to social networks to "read" the word on the street. Guest reviews on TripAdvisor, for instance, have become a daily must-read for many hotel managers, and the smart ones respond to each one directly. One of the fastest-growing e-commerce fashion retailers to emerge in a decade is built on a model of very personal interactions with its shopping community. Using online outreach programs to gauge precisely what buyers want and to supply only what people are buying, ModCloth has gone from its one-woman launch in a home basement to a reported $100 million in sales, 450 full-time employees and offices in Los

Angeles, San Francisco and Pittsburg. And the ModCloth story is not unique: a recent *Forbes* report estimates that customers reward companies that have a social media presence with 64 percent more business, and almost a third of companies with a social media presence report higher profit margins. Twitter itself has benefited immensely from the ecosystem of its own users. Twitter didn't invent the retweet, or even the hashtag. Both were dreamed up by savvy users of the platform in 2007 and are now among the most widely used forms of distributing information on Twitter. These kinds of consumer-driven initiatives, whether co-creation, crowdsourcing or customization of everything from clothes to cars, has become a hot trend. When CEOs of the fastest-growing private companies in the US, as ranked by the 2014 survey of the Inc. 500, were asked where they go for ideas, 28 percent said they go to their customers. It's increasingly a bespoke world, custom-tailored for individual tastes and needs.

In today's environment, there's just no telling where inspiration will come from. But to tap into the possibilities, leaders have to bring a wide-open mind. Companies may once have had the luxury of creating strategic plans to take them through the next five years or more. Today, attempting to project out even two years seems crazy. When people ask me where TV will be in five years, I say, "Who knew Netflix would be winning Golden Globes and shutting out the traditional networks?" Yet just because it's harder to see far down the road doesn't mean you shouldn't know from the get-go where you'd like to end up. Having a vision and long-term goals are still crucial to building any solid career or business. But adhering to a pre-formulated plan on your way to reaching those goals—*because it's the plan*—limits your opportunities.

Which is why most of our client meetings at Twitter usually involved epic brainstorms where we and the clients would imagine together what a campaign might look like. Maybe we wouldn't get the deal. But, more often than not, we did. And by doing it this way, we didn't just build a client list, we built relationships. Clients trusted us to try things out. Sometimes our ideas worked, sometimes they didn't. But when the relationship was there, they would come back for another shot whether we succeeded or failed. The same trust we'd engendered internally in our team extended to our clients and partners. In the two years I led the Canadian office, we grew from nothing into a thriving enterprise, and Canada became one of the highest revenue-generating regions in Twitter's global operations. I did not do it alone. My success had everything to do with the team, and the collaborative approach that's now also essential to my new management role as Twitter's vice-president of Media, North America. Leveraging content related to news, sports and entertainment, I head up a team of more than fifty employees who never go to an office together—*ever*. My team that handles government news is based in Washington, DC. The TV and film team runs out of Los Angeles and the crew involved in sports, news, music and entertainment works where I do now, out of Twitter's New York offices. When we do get together it's often to work at major events, as we did in Phoenix, for instance, at the 2015 Super Bowl, and then again at the Oscars and the NBA All-Star weekend. (It's my version of visiting the factory floor, because our product—which is content—originates on-site.) While I was at the Super Bowl, our sports team liaised with our partners, journalists and the NFL, helping them get out the game highlights, behind-the-scenes colour and commentary, and related tweets from viewers and players. But outside of such big public events, the only regular face time I have with my team is through a screen: video conferencing. Otherwise it's text, DM, gchat, tweet, email and phone calls. I'm not there to lord it over them or tell anyone what to do at any microlevel. They are the experts in their field. My role is to listen to their best information, communicate the company's overall goals and offer my knowledge and guidance as we craft an ever-developing strategy to reach our aims.

Our job is to set up people for success. How they choose to use Twitter is completely up to them. We treat our partners with the same respect I give my team. I offer guidance and the right tools, then I get the heck out of the way to let them do what they do best. There's nothing Mr. Burns about it.

Influence Is the New Power

SO MANY OF THE DECISIONS THAT matter most today are made by a group. Collaboration has never been more critical to leadership, whether it's among internal teams or with clients. Managing "out" is the new key to innovation. Yet for eons, the chiefs among us—from tribes to boardrooms—have operated on the principle that power is personal; you don't share it, you wield it. That style worked in a time when power belonged to the few people in the know and information would only be doled out as needed to accompany marching orders—or not even then. But now being "in the know" is just a Google search away. Information as power has lost its currency. Today it's not *having* the information that counts, it's what you do with it. It's not having the answers, but knowing which questions to ask that makes you a leader. "Understanding 'New Power,'" a hugely influential article by Jeremy Heimans (co-founder of Purpose, which has been called the "mothership of movement-building") and Henry Timms (executive director of New York's 92nd Street Y and instigator of #GivingTuesday), published in the December 2014 issue of the *Harvard Business Review,* nailed the distinction between old ways of power and new: "old power" worked like a currency—held by a few, jealously guarded and leader-driven—where "new power" operates more like a current, made by many, participatory, peer-driven, and most forceful when it surges. It's not to be stockpiled, but channelled.

Working my way up from the corporate bottom, I learned from the leaders and managers above me that those who kept information and the power to make decisions to themselves were soon overwhelmed and, in the worst of times, paralysed. Since they didn't bring their people into the circle of information, their people couldn't do their part to handle a task and then that task was badly handled. There was danger, too, when leaders only tapped people they liked, creating an inner circle of their friends as opposed to seeking out those who could do the job best. In its worst manifestations, such a leadership style creates an emperor-has-no-clothes scenario, leaders surrounding themselves with the nodding heads of old boys' clubs and protective circles of mean girls. A successful, modern leader doesn't need a cheerleading squad. Quite the opposite. The first thing a leader needs is the trust, respect and support of her team, because trust encourages constructive criticism, disagreement and healthy debate. And though trust and respect is a two-way street built between leader and team, it's up to leaders to set the example. A leader's transparency can be shocking for some and a refreshing change for others. But it's a necessary first step to building a healthy relationship with a team. It takes guts to share information, the good and the bad, and to trust a team to do its best with it. But in today's world the risk you take by trying to go it alone as a leader isn't worth it, especially when it causes you to ignore the wealth of brainpower you can harness when you are open.

It has been hard for women in particular to share power; we've had it so rarely, the last thing we want to do is let it get away. And when information is power, sometimes we hold it back with the belief that we can handle a matter ourselves. I know I've often assumed that I could manage a situation solo, when I could have benefited by bringing other bright minds to bear. Sometimes we don't share because we underestimate the significance of our knowledge or don't recognize that we actually do have valuable information to contribute. That young woman who approached me after my talk at the Rotman School, for instance, likely had a whole wealth of valuable data points that were being missed because she felt she could only provide answers to questions the sales team asked. Yet how much more valuable would her research be if she served up the answers to questions they never knew to ask? How much personal capital would she build by allowing the team to benefit from her insights?

Information moves at high speeds and volatility rules the markets. Data about trends, opportunities, the competition, about customers and from customers, flies in around the clock from everywhere. And it demands the attention of a nimble team to digest it because any of it might require action. The kind of leader who is going to excel under these conditions doesn't keep knowledge under lock and key, but sets it out in the wild for her team to absorb, analyze and interpret. The modern leader's role is to appreciate the information flooding in from multiple inputs and then to consult with the team to figure out the best way forward. Ultimately, it remains the job of the leader to act. But today, the only way to build power is to share power, because leadership is not really about exercising power at all. It's about influence.

The old ways of working centred on the idea of power as the key to maintaining control. But having control is a vain hope today. People resist being led by fear and don't want to work for companies that don't have their best interests at heart. The best you can aim for is the capacity to indirectly shape people's opinions and behaviours because they believe what you say, what you stand for and see you and your organization as trustworthy. The global village doesn't judge companies on their bottom lines and, increasingly, not even on their brands, but on their authenticity, their reputations and the integrity of their interactions with the people they serve. The more empathic, innovative and responsive a company is, the more influence they are likely to wield. Which is why I think we're about to see a meaningful breakthrough in the numbers of women in leadership roles. Those qualities the market now demands of its companies and corporations are traits long considered "feminine." Caliper, the Princeton-based talent management company, recently studied the personal attributes of male and female leaders from nineteen different business sectors. The research, which included in-depth interviews with fifty-nine women from top companies in the US and the UK, such as Bank of America, Deloitte & Touche, Deutsche Bank, The Economist Group, IBM, Kohler, Molson Coors and several others, found that women scored significantly higher than men on sociability, flexibility, the ability to read situations, build consensus and form strategy—and form it quickly.

If we women can get over the temptation to hide what we know, or what we think, and put it out there, we have precisely what it takes to lead today: an aptitude for synthesizing information from many sources, anticipating needs and appreciating various viewpoints, even those contrary to our own. What's more, as research has also shown, women are particularly strong at encouraging others to share their views and contribute their creative energies for the betterment of the team. And that's the deal-breaker. Because what hasn't changed amid the seismic shifts of the information age—what has only become more important—is that any organization is only going to be as strong as the teams who work for them. Today, it's all about *the people*.

Growing the New

IN THE KNOWLEDGE ECONOMY, human capital is the asset that matters the most. When the world's leading hotelier, taxi company, retailer and information provider owns no hotels, no taxis, no stores, or publications, it's not a leap to conclude that what's crucial for any enterprise to succeed are *ideas*—and those don't roll off the old assembly lines. You have to grow ideas, and that means first clearing a field, planting the seeds and then nurturing them. The right leaders for success today know to rule not by law but by motivation: giving people a voice, respecting individual values and encouraging brainstorming to create an environment where it's safe to experiment, and propose new, even unorthodox, ideas. Leading today is not about what the boss thinks, but how the boss responds, and the more input a leader can draw from a dynamic and eclectic team, the better that response will be.

According to the Center for Talent Innovation, this is another area where women have an advantage because they're naturals at fostering these kinds of innovative teams. Its research, based on 1,800 survey responses and interviews with dozens of executives, team leaders and employees at Fortune 500 companies, finds the kind of leaders most likely to create these inclusive, speak-up cultures are those who keenly appreciate the value of different perspectives because they themselves are different from the traditional leader—as in non-European, under thirty-five, or female. In short, mix it up at the top and those bolts of brilliance are more likely to shoot up from the bottom: bolts that might well pay big dividends. When business professors at the University of Maryland and Columbia University studied the effect of gender diversity on top companies in the S&P Composite 1500 list, they found that firms that prioritized innovation saw greater financial gains when women were part of the top leadership ranks.

I think a woman's leadership strength comes from our general inclination to want to do not just a decent job, but the best job we can do. While we might sometimes be inclined to play our cards close to the vest, we're also usually comfortable admitting what we don't know and reaching out to our networks of people to find the information we need. If it means assembling the best team and ignoring the conventional company structure to figure things out, as I did at the CBC to prep our coverage for the Sochi Olympics, that's what we'll do. If you want to encourage innovation or solve a problem, then gathering multiple perspectives and creating teams diverse in background and in ideas is the best way to get it. Input from different cultures, genders and generations usually brings constructive challenges to the status quo. Diversity is as good for a garden as it is for business— not just to be socially conscious, but to stay competitive. If your firm is filled with people who all have the same backgrounds and tend to share the same opinions, chances are, as the folks at Nokia learned the hard way, opportunities will be missed. A recent article in the *Guardian* told the story of Beam, the bourbon company whose net profits soared to a record high of $2.5 billion in 2012 after it acquired Skinnygirl Cocktails, a line of premixed drinks created by reality-TV star Bethenny Frankel. She had approached all the major liquor companies, run mostly by males, and they had turned her down flat, so she decided to go it alone. Frankel went on to sell so many cases that the men from Beam came to her, offering $39 million for the brand. It was a stunning example of how the largely male-run liquor companies had missed a major market opportunity by thinking they knew their customers best. But it's hardly the only evidence that firms lacking diversity are losing out.

A *Harvard Business Review* study from 2013, involving 1,800 professionals, found that employees of firms with true diversity were 45 percent more likely to report a growth in market share over the previous year, and 70 percent more likely to report the capture of a new market. A diverse company simply has a better shot at connecting with global markets that are only becoming ever more diverse. In Canada today we have four generations working together for the first time in history (the Silent Generation, Boomers, Gen X and Gen Y), and a visible-minority population growing five times faster than the increase for the population as a whole, according to the 2006 Canadian census. In the US, the Census Bureau predicts minorities will be the majority by 2042. And when it comes to gender diversity, companies have every reason to include more women in their teams, not just because women drive about, oh, 80 percent of all purchasing decisions, make up half the population and, morally, it's just the right thing to do. But because it's the smart thing to do. There's a growing body of compelling research that shows including women makes groups smarter.

Psychologists from Carnegie Mellon, MIT and Union College recently completed a fascinating series of studies to examine whether some groups, like some individuals, are reliably smarter than others. They assembled 697 volunteers, grouped them into teams of two to five, and gave each team a series of tasks designed to reflect real-world problems, tasks that involved brainstorming, logical analysis, and others that focused on coordination and moral reasoning.

They found groups that did well on one task did well on others too. When they tried to figure out what made these teams "smarter" they were surprised by what they found. The successful teams weren't filled with high-IQ members or packed with extroverts or keeners who raised the level of collective intelligence. Rather, the smart teams were those where members contributed to the group discussions equally, as opposed to having one or two dominate. Members of the smart teams scored higher on a visual test designed to measure how well the volunteers could read the emotions of others just by looking at facial images in which only the eyes were visible (a test called "Reading the Mind in the Eyes"). The teams with more women outperformed teams with more men—and the more women a team had, the better they performed. This, the researchers concluded, had a lot to do with the fact women outscored men on the emotional intelligence "mind-reading" test.

But what was just as surprising—and incredibly relevant given the way our tech world works—is that the researchers discovered in a follow-up study that this result held true even when the teams worked exclusively online. As they wrote earlier this year in a much-discussed piece in the *New York Times*, "Emotion-reading mattered just as much for the online teams whose members could not see one another as for the teams that worked face to face." And once again the upshot was the same: women were consistently better at reading between the lines to interpret other people's emotions, which, in turn, was a key factor in how well the team performed.

As this kind of evidence mounts, so does the urgency to recruit more women at all levels in the corporate world. And for women, who can often be hesitant to step up and speak out, there's never been a better time to be heard.

I'm the Boss of Me

AS MUCH AS RECRUITING the right team is essential to success, holding on to that talent is crucial for survival. If leaders don't create an environment that fosters employee engagement and empowerment, their people will up and leave them for the competition. The race for good people, and women especially, is fierce and global.

I think one major frustration that can make employees bolt from a job is feeling irrelevant. Just as leadership characteristics are changing, so is employee culture. When bosses ruled by decree, employees were accustomed to following the rules, ready to receive and deliver on their marching orders, keeping their opinions to themselves if they hoped to keep their jobs. It wasn't long ago that dictatorial memos from the boss were met with resigned silence. Today that sort of top-down, one-way relationship seems as ludicrous as Mr. Burns. Now, when I send a note to the team, an excited chain of responses greets it, ranging from *"Agree +1"* to *"Is this what we really want to do as a company?"* As a leader you not only have to be ready to deal with those responses, you should encourage them. Nothing puts a wedge between leader and team more than the thought that one doesn't care about the other. Nothing is more demoralizing than to think your opinion doesn't matter. Creating an environment where differences are respected is one of the most important things a leader can foster to ensure success.

What matters to modern employees is to feel that they're making a meaningful contribution, that they have purpose and a stake in the work they do, and a certain amount of autonomy in how it gets done. The importance of meaningful work is bound to increase as younger generations make their way through the workforce. People in their twenties and thirties right now have been raised to speak their minds, to have and share opinions, and to be listened to and accommodated when they do. And technology, along with this generational rise, is driving this cultural shift too.

After all, if technology has brought us anything, it is the freedom and flexibility to manage ourselves, our tasks and our time. When neither time nor place is an impediment to communicating, it makes *you* the boss of you—able to wear many hats at once, engage in several conversations simultaneously, resolve scheduling conflicts between work and home, and work where and when we can.

From a logistical standpoint this has been a boon, especially for women, making the eternal work–life juggle just that much easier to handle. While this is also true for men who, increasingly, are doing more on the home front, the conflict between family and work has traditionally been the most stubborn barrier that holds women back professionally. I remember when I had to return to work early after my first child was born, getting home on time was crucial. But my job was also vital to me, and to my family, since I was the sole earner. I spent many afternoons with one eye on the person talking too long at the last meeting of the day, and one eye on the door that would lead to the 5:55 p.m. train that would take me home to my baby. I learned how to sprint. Sometimes I made it, but often

I didn't. It never got easier, even as the girls got older. But then BlackBerry saved me. I could join the meeting on the ride home. I could answer questions from the ice rink where my youngest practised. I could step out briefly from the school play that I would have missed if I hadn't been able to be on call.

Phone mobility set me free, as it has many people juggling busy lives at home and work. Now you can be home with a sick child and Skype a meeting, offer feedback from a taxi, review a document while making dinner, or help your daughter with homework while en route from LA to Toronto (@AirCanada Wi-Fi, thank you). I think of my smartphone as a lifeline, connecting me to family in ways never before possible. Messaging has become the tool that keeps us in close touch, especially when I travel. And I travel a lot. Nothing says parental peace of mind quite like a ping from home. My girls send messages to let me know their plans, or that they've made it home safely, or to make "urgent" announcements, as when my youngest iMessaged me to tell me exactly what she wanted for her sweet sixteen party—when she was fourteen.

These days, work is not somewhere you *go*; it's something you *do*. And what we do in the knowledge economy is contribute our knowledge, our thoughts and ideas, or what makes us curious—wherever and whenever that happens. Increasingly, it means that individuals are assessed by their performance, not their presence. After all, younger generations, whose social lives are already deeply embedded in the digital media, will only be more likely to want to live their professional lives the same way. Already, research finds that Gen Y favours telecommuting not only for the work–life freedom it brings, but for the environmental benefits of being able to skip commutes and reduce vehicle emissions. As it is, the number of people working outside a traditional office is rising dramatically in the global village. Forecasts from the International Data Corporation, a multinational market intelligence firm, suggest the mobile worker population is expected to reach 1.3 billion this year, representing 37.2 percent of the total global workforce. And the Telework Research Network projected in 2013 that the mobile workforce will increase 63 percent over the next five years.

But it's taking time for businesses to recognize employee value isn't measured by hours sitting at a desk. (I think we've all felt that judgement when a manager assumes if you're not chained to the desk, you're not working.) But there's a growing recognition that employers have a lot to gain from allowing workers to work remotely: overhead savings, time otherwise lost in commutes, fewer sick days and higher productivity. Research shows telecommuters tend to work more efficiently, with fewer distractions and greater focus. A 2013 Citrix study showed 18 percent of small businesses in the United States, Canada and Australia are enjoying a 30 percent increase in productivity through the adoption of mobile work styles. And a 2011 WORKshift Canada report concluded employers can save more than $10,000 per year for every employee who telecommutes only two days each week.

But perhaps the most compelling reason to support a mobile workforce is that it makes for happier employees. And happier employees are less likely to leave than those who are office-bound. A 2013 BMO study on telecommuting found that 64 percent of Canadian businesses surveyed saw a positive impact on morale and the ability to entice and retain high-quality employees. A 2010 Telus poll indicated 67 percent of Canadians surveyed would be more loyal to a company offering remote working flexibility. I'd argue that companies that might never have considered telecommuting, job sharing, flextime or compressed weeks now can't afford not to do so (though of course this doesn't apply to all occupations, such as teaching or jobs in the service industry).

At Twitter, and at a lot of tech companies, there are no limits on vacation time. Employees are free to take off as many weeks per year as they like so long as their work is complete, and they've reached their specific goals or targets. An unlimited vacation policy is one that some find as hard to believe in as the free breakfasts, lunches and drinks available for all Twitter employees. (I almost cried when I first took in the daily spread, fresh from the tight-pursed public-sector culture of the CBC where in the last round of cuts I'd slashed the bottled water.) And Twitter's generous employee benefits are not unique. A growing number of companies offer perks around meals and vacation time to encourage company loyalty and keep teams focused on their goals.

There's a valid concern that technology may enslave as much as liberate us, keep us tied to our jobs day and night. I get that. I've been caught out by my family in certain moments when my phone stole time from them. I remember looking up from it at the rink one afternoon, where my daughter was doing her training for speed skating, and there she stood pointing up at me in the stands, that one little index finger calling me out to pay attention! Ultimately, using the freedom technology can give us comes down to understanding your limits, knowing when to floor it and when to put on the brakes: again, flow, not balance. In many ways, technological innovation has forced the trend of managing out and spreading "on call" time more evenly across a team. When the BlackBerry made its debut while I was working at Hallmark in the early 2000s, I remember how it changed the culture of expectation. Suddenly there was a sense that everyone was always reachable, particularly in the non-stop news business and with several channels in several countries. I felt a new responsibility not to make people in other time zones wait to hear my decision before they could move ahead. For a while, I lost a whole lot of sleep and a bit of my sanity. But over time, I learned to delegate and deputize people, so that I was no longer the only decision-maker, or the place where a decision might be held up. Tech prompted me to share power and empower. And that's a philosophy I've carried forward to today, in my new role leading multiple team members scattered across multiple time zones. Like it or not, and mostly I like it enormously, I am at the cutting edge of a new way of working in the world.

VIII

Thriving at the Edge of
the Glass Cliff

FOR SIX MONTHS BEFORE I was officially hired to head up
the CBC, I was already doing the job. Richard Stursberg
had left abruptly in August 2010, and I pinch-hit while the
CBC brass looked for his replacement. Having had a successful four-year run in charge of television programming, I'd
heard I was a candidate for the job. But I also heard that
the president's outside headhunters were shopping around,
worried that I didn't have the "gravitas" to take the helm. To
quote US talk show host Katie Couric, who heard a similar
comment about her at *CBS Evening News*, "gravitas" is Latin
for "testicles."

I have no idea how many candidates sporting gravitas
were interviewed to become executive vice-president before
I was appointed, or how many applied. I did hear that men
who might have been interested were less so because the job
came with an absence of perks and a plethora of big responsibilities with a salary that wasn't, intense scrutiny, low

morale, high expectations, competition growing by the click and budget cuts looming. A dream job, right? Still, despite all the cons, I believed I had something worth giving and this was my shot to give it—and at the CBC, quite possibly the only one I'd have. Whatever stars aligned to finally convince the decision-makers that I had the right stuff to become the first woman to head up Canada's national broadcaster, I may never know. What I do know is that the decision to install a woman in the corner office when a company is struggling is a common one. It's so common that in management and academic circles it's known as "the glass cliff."

Researchers at England's University of Exeter coined the term in 2004 after a report in a British newspaper suggested that hiring women to lead is bad for business. The *Times* of London had run an exposé the year before linking the appointment of female board members to the poor health of a hundred of Britain's biggest firms, prompting one pundit to write: "the triumphant march of women into the country's boardrooms has wreaked havoc on companies' performance and share prices." But Exeter psychologists Michelle Ryan and Alex Haslam had a closer look at the data and found that the women had not caused the companies to struggle, rather, the women were brought in *after* the firms had been struggling. Companies that had consistently poor performance with overall stock market declines were found to be more likely to appoint women to their boards; firms enjoying a period of share-price stability were more apt to appoint men. Writing in the *British Journal of Management* in 2005, the researchers concluded that women were more likely to be promoted to power during troubled times when the chances of failing are highest. In other words, women who manage to break through the glass ceiling often find themselves on the edge of a glass cliff, where there's a strong risk of falling off. Other studies have found evidence that the glass cliff applies to ethnic minorities as well as women. Christy Glass and Alison Cook at Utah State University found the trend among Fortune 500 companies and NCAA Division I basketball coaches (visible minorities were much more likely to be promoted to coach losing teams). So whether it's in the realm of business, sports or politics, it seems that women, or visible-minority men and women, are more likely to be tapped to lead when the going gets tough.

Not everyone buys the theory, and there are plenty of examples of male chief executives thrust into a hot seat. But anecdotally at least, the glass-cliff pattern seems dead easy to spot: The US elected Barack Obama, its first black president, in the midst of one of the worst economic crises in the country's history. Kim Campbell, Canada's first and very short-lived female prime minister, came to power on the eve of the Conservative Party's destruction at the polls. Iceland, in the wake of its stunning economic meltdown, elected its first female prime minister, Jóhanna Sigurðardóttir, and the world's first openly lesbian head of state, to lead the rescue.

In the corporate world, there's Mary Barra, who kicked off her tenure as the first woman to run General Motors mired in an ignition-switch crisis linked to at least twenty-one deaths, a thirty-million-car recall and a congressional inquiry. Sunoco ushered in Lynn L. Elsenhans, its first female chief executive, after its share prices had fallen about 52 percent. The first woman to lead Xerox, Anne Mulcahy, was promoted to CEO when it was under investigation by the US Securities and Exchange Commission and $17 billion in debt. Even Yahoo's decision to hire Marissa Mayer was made at a time when the company was in dire need of fixing. A *Forbes* headline after her appointment read, "Did Marissa Mayer just receive the job offer of a lifetime or did she just ascend to the pinnacle of the glass cliff?"

The Upside of Down

SO WHY OPT for a woman at the top when an organization has hit the skids? I'd suspect that part of the motivation is a subtle sexist inclination to set women up for failure. Put a female in charge when she's likely to flop, and if she does, she proves that a woman was never up to the task of leading. If, against the odds, she succeeds, great. Either way the firm looks like a progressive, equal opportunity shop. It's a cynical perspective; though some evidence suggests it's not a fictional one. There's been speculation from *The Huffington Post* to *The Hindustan Times* as to whether Jill Abramson, who was fired as the first female editor of the *New York Times* after just two years on the job, was a victim of it (though she was replaced by the paper's first black editor-in-chief). Researchers at Utah State found that women and minorities promoted during a crisis are allotted a year less time to show results than a male leader in the same position. In short, if the outliers don't turn things around in a heartbeat they're shoved off that glass cliff and often replaced by a traditional leader—literally, a white knight. Researchers have dubbed it "the saviour effect."

(I certainly felt the implied question mark when a headline after I took over at the public broadcaster screamed, "Queen Ceeb, Saviour of the CBC.")

But aside from old-boys'-club biases, I think there are other, more instructive dynamics at work when women are chosen to lead in troubled times. For starters, who a company hires has a lot to do with who lines up for the job. It's my sense that women may be more inclined to take on a riskier, less appealing job. Men tend to want immediate results. They're more interested in leadership positions with the seeds of success already sown in. Trying to lead a corporation out of a tailspin is messy. Like when you clean out an old desk drawer, you have to take everything out and sort through what's worth keeping before you can reorganize it, and you could end up looking at a much bigger mess.

I think women are more comfortable with that; for women, life is often messy. We often have to deal with other people's needs and emotions, a multitude of demands and deadlines. Every day is a bit like cleaning out the desk drawer. You take stock of what's on the agenda, figure out what you can fit in when and what you have to let go. I think men are also less inclined to clean up someone else's mess. Not only does it take too long to get results, the risk of failure is too high and so is the possibility that a failure marked against your name could damage your leadership prospects for a long time to come. Women tend to measure success a bit differently. Given that less than 5 percent of Fortune 500 company chief executives are female, I'd say the rare opportunity for a woman to finally break through the glass ceiling outweighs the risk of failure. That's how I felt about the big

CBC job: This is the shot that you've got. You might fall flat on your face, but you might not. And if you don't give it what you can, you'll never know what you can do.

Too often we women don't put our hands up for things—assignments, positions or promotions—unless we're absolutely positively sure we can handle it. But if we're going to test ourselves to our limits, we have to trust our ability to make things work, a point I'll explore more in the final chapter. More of us should put our hands up, vie for the risky positions and promotions. We shouldn't shy away from the cliffs, we should seek them out, and stand tall on the edge. Was I apprehensive about taking on the mammoth task of modernizing a coast-to-coast multimedia company of five thousand employees? You bet. At that moment, there was no doubting where I stood, right on the edge of a slippery and jagged precipice. But it only made me more determined to dig in my heels (yes, the high kind).

And here's the less cynical perspective: there are many good reasons for companies in crisis to ask a woman to steer the ship out of the storm. When an organization is faring well, it's reluctant to rock the boat; better to stay the course, and hire "the expected." When it's adrift or sinking in a financial or public relations storm, the status quo is already out the window and it's logical to opt for change: to choose a new kind of leader and chart a new course. Putting a woman or a leader from a visible minority at the helm sends a clear and instant message that change is afoot simply by virtue of the leader *not being* male or white. My initial entry at the CBC made waves in part because I looked nothing like leaders who had come before. And I believe there's a growing recognition, backed by research, and dazzling examples, that women are well suited to lead when times get tough.

The first female chief executives at Sunoco and Xerox have both been widely credited for turning their companies' fortunes around. Even Mary Barra at GM, who started her historic tenure with profuse apologies for faulty ignition switches, earned kudos for her forthright handling of the crisis, launching an internal investigation and promising to regain the public's trust. And Ellen Kullman, who was named the first female CEO of DuPont when earnings at the 212-year-old company had plummeted, increased those earnings by 24 percent in three years, landing her on *Fortune* magazine's top 50 list of the world's greatest leaders.

It Really Is Our Turn

NO ONE LIKES TO BE PUT IN A BOX or described as a set of typical qualities, but there are attributes traditionally held to be "feminine" traits whether we're born with them, learn them or both. For years in the workplace, these qualities put women neatly into a corner, but not the corner office. Take multi-tasking. A woman's ability to do more than one thing at a time indicated a problem: she lacked focus. Or worse: she had to do so many things because people gave her all the tasks. Women's tendencies to be sensitive and empathetic, good communicators and listeners who could anticipate the needs of others: these were seen as "soft skills" suited to support staff, but not vital for success at a senior level. But today, all those characteristics that confined women to the low rungs of corporate ladders are now seen as tickets to the corner

office. A wide range of management studies, involving interviews with hundreds of executives from different countries
and industries, are finding that traditionally feminine traits
are now at the core of successful modern leadership.

There are signs, albeit modest, that this is translating into
real advancement for women: Female chief executives are
still incredibly rare, but their numbers are growing and the
trend is predicted to accelerate, according to the 2013 Chief
Executive Study from Strategy&, the global management
consulting arm of PricewaterhouseCoopers. Examining 14
years of data on the turnover of CEOs at 2,500 of the world's
largest public companies, the study predicts that women will
make up a third of CEOs by 2040. What's more, companies
have been going out of their way to hire women: women
were more likely than men to be recruited to the position of
CEO from outside a firm than from within it. That might
partly reflect an absence of women in senior positions within
a company who might make worthy candidates. But I believe
that companies are now coming to appreciate the value that
a woman leader has to offer.

At its heart, leading effectively has as much to do with
reading people as reading spreadsheets. Over the years, I've
worked for many impressively brilliant bosses and while I love
working for smart bosses, a high IQ without the presence of a
healthy EQ isn't good enough today. And here again, women
shine: studies consistently show that females have an edge in
matters of reading and interpreting the emotions of others. A
2014 European study of more than 4,600 people, for instance,
found that women outperformed men in almost all aspects of
emotional intelligence, including understanding, facilitating

and managing emotions. Bottom line: women know how to build bridges over troubled waters. Women tend to be better communicators, and better at building communities. I can't tell you how many times I have been asked to step up and translate a boss's message or idea to the wider group. It's why the role of spokesperson often fell to me. I'm someone who had worked her way up, and I relate to the teams at any level, because at different points in my career I've also experienced what they were going through.

Of course leading is not just about the ablility to communicate, but what you communicate. Talk the talk, sure, but you better be able to walk the walk. Since women score highly in many studies when it comes to mentoring, motivating and mobilizing people to contribute, create and innovate, they are primed to lead in times where a turnaround is necessary. A 2012 Dutch study from the University of Groningen (which also found women are overrepresented in leadership roles during a crisis) concluded that "feminine" qualities are most desirable when an organization is in peril. The study found that men prefer to exert hierarchy and authority to solve problems, whereas women rely on tact and understanding to manage workplace turmoil.

There's also a belief that seeing a woman at the helm signals a less aggressive and more healing approach, softer, humbler, more collaborative and reasoned, which is exactly what you want if your company is on the cliff, fractured and floundering, has to publicly apologize, or dig its way out of debt. Last year, the *Cambridge Journal of Economics* published "The Lehman Sisters Hypothesis," which by title alone essentially suggests the mostly male-led Wall Street firm might have survived if it had had more women at the top. As those glass-cliff researchers from Exeter found, companies that did appoint a woman during a financial downturn actually experienced a marked increase in share price after the appointment. Yet despite all this, we tend to underappreciate the value we can bring to corner offices. In one of the most influential reports on the perceptions of gender and leadership, a meta-analysis of nearly a hundred studies published in 2014, researchers from the College of Business at Florida International University found that while men rate themselves as being significantly more effective leaders than women rate themselves, other people rate women as significantly more effective than men.

The hard lesson in all of this is that women have to learn to see their natural talents as powerful leadership assets. Flex those muscles and understand how effective they can be. Too often, we keep our heads down, do the grunt work and keep our thoughts to ourselves, hoarding our knowledge like nuts for a winter that might never come. But here's the thing: winter has arrived. This is the moment to present ourselves as leaders, to speak up and vocalize our vision. There's profound opportunity here. These are volatile, and vulnerable, times. Women have what it takes to lead from that proverbial cliff, and those cliffs are everywhere now.

Fearlessly Uncertain

THE RAPID SPREAD OF digital technology has disrupted, and in some cases, destroyed, the business model in many sectors of the economy. Media, music, publishing, retail, travel, finance, banking, health care: it's practically impossible to think of an industry where technology hasn't changed the game. Profit margins are being squeezed. Competition has grown and gone global. Revenue streams are drying up and many companies, even long-standing, storied institutions, have been caught off guard. Just keeping internal systems current is a challenge. Even companies who saw change coming are scrambling to adapt, and that's no easy feat when there's no clear way forward. No one knows what strategies will fly or fail when change is the only constant. In this environment, who isn't leading from a cliff?

The only way to find a solid footing today is to explore new paths, and once again this is where I believe women also have a certain advantage. Women tend to be fearless in the ways that matter most in today's climate of uncertainty. In a time when information and data rule the day, being fearless often means admitting what it is you don't know. It's risky to forge ahead, blind to the possibilities hidden in the wealth of data that swirls around us. In 2010, before the GPS became ubiquitous, Sheilas' Wheels, a British car insurance firm, actually investigated if there was any truth to the stereotype that men hate to ask for directions, and found that men in the UK drive an average of 276 extra miles per year because they'd rather be lost than have a stranger point the way. (A quarter of the men polled said they'd drive around for half an hour before asking. A stubborn 12 percent said they'd never ask.)

The corollary to this is that women are more comfortable asking (three-quarters of them, according to the study) because women are less likely to see asking for help as a show of weakness. If we need assistance to complete a task or get where we're going, we ask for it. (Another study from Exeter found that women would be less likely to take a precarious, glass-cliff job if it lacked social resources such as employee support; for men the deal-breaker was a lack of financial resources.)

For me, having repeatedly been the outsider recruited to shake things up or build something new, plotting the way forward always starts with stepping into the unknown, while relying on those who are already there to help me navigate. Unlike some male leaders I've witnessed, I've never thought that the only way forward is to obliterate the existing landscape. At Hallmark, when I realized I lacked information about audience tastes in the various countries, I worked with the head of research to commission studies to get it. At Twitter, when I was building the Canadian business from scratch, I tapped into the knowledge and insights of the new team, just as they tapped into mine. Asking people for input can set in motion a healthy chain of events in the workplace by countering those negative feelings that many employees have around feeling irrelevant. When you ask people to share their opinions or insights, you reinforce the message that you value what they know. If you act on what you hear from them, it signals that what they contribute counts. To see formerly alienated teams come alive after they finally see that their work matters is a thrilling thing.

Of course people can sometimes be reluctant to contribute, worried that they will wear the blame if an idea or strategy backfires. And I understand that apprehension. I've been there. When I was at Alliance Atlantis I had a pivotal moment where I felt that I'd been unfairly left holding the bag. We had been looking for ways to increase revenues at the Food Network with programs that would broaden our audience:

it was all about pushing margins. My boss at the time suggested that I take a look at our CRTC description to see if it gave us any flexibility on the kinds of shows we could air. The Canadian Radio-television and Telecommunications Commission, the independent public authority that regulates broadcasters in Canada, had set out rules for our operation and among them was a very small programming allowance suggesting that we could show movies so long as they were food related. So we went ahead and added movies to our Sunday night time slot, features such as *Chocolat* and *Eat Drink Man Woman*. But not for long. The CRTC came down on us with a strict warning: we had misinterpreted the clause and would face consequences if we didn't stop. Suddenly my boss and the head of communications developed short-term memory loss, forgetting this was a decision we made together, and in a meeting called me out for *my* mistake. I was livid. I was embarrassed. I felt abandoned and I vowed to never leave anyone hanging in the way they had left me. As a leader, in times of crisis, failure or mistake, the buck stops with you. Every leader along the chain should feel that kind of responsibility so that the entire team is supported from all angles. We are in this together and to shirk responsibility or, worse, assign blame only serves to teach a team not to reach so far next time because there is no net to catch you if you slip. At one time or another, we all do slip.

Of course, no one *likes* to take responsibility for bad decisions or bad news. But being brave enough to communicate fearlessly in good times and bad is essential if you hope to foster a healthy environment where everyone does the same. There were too many times in my TV career where people haven't been brave enough to own up to the fact that they were part of a decision-making process that resulted in a hard-to-swallow or unpopular call. Programming decisions were made in an open discussion where all executives weighed in before we reached a consensus and a call was finalized. Yet when one of those executives had to deliver bad news and let the cast or producers know that a show was to be rescheduled or dropped, too many times they would fold and dodge: "Yeah, sorry, I loved it but 'the boss' says no." Or a producer would want to make a creative cast or crew change, and ask for our backing, then tell the person who was being fired, "Sorry, network says we have to."

Not owning your decisions creates an environment of distress at all levels. The people hearing the bad news lose faith in the executive, who now appears to have no clout or influence. Worse, they lose faith in an organization that looks like it's being run arbitrarily from the top. And eventually, the boss finds out, as I invariably did, that the executive shirked responsibility for a decision they were a pivotal part of, and the boss loses trust in the executive, who then really does lose trust and influence. Leaders undermine their own ability to lead when they want to play the nice guy and pass the blame on.

That sour experience at Alliance Atlantis taught me an important lesson about the value of integrity in leadership, one that I feel is critical in creating the kind of open culture needed to succeed today. When so much depends on innovation, on out-of-the-box ideas, every team member has to feel comfortable and confident pitching theirs. They have to feel the leader has their back and they won't be punished for things that don't always work out the way you hoped. Even in failure, there's something to be learned and that lesson can inform the next move you make. A leader has to make sure their team understands that's how your shop rolls. And creating that culture of trust and solidarity can begin with the smallest of gestures, which is also something I learned from a boss. On my first trip abroad for Paragon with Isme Bennie, I ordered breakfast to my room, and a yogurt and orange juice arrived along with a bill for $35. I nearly choked. I thought, "I am going to get fired the first day of my first business trip." But when I told her what happened, apologized and offered to pay the bill, she just looked at me and said, "No, you won't pay. You're here on business. You have to eat. That's what things cost here. It's the cost of doing business."

I went on to generate hundreds of thousands of dollars in revenue on that trip. Good ROI. But that's not what stuck with me. It was what Isme had said. It may sound like an insignificant exchange, but to me it set a standard of decency and mutual respect I'd like to think I've carried with me ever since. Those small gestures are essential to building strong workplace relationships: sending flowers when someone's had a baby, remembering to write a note of congratulations, hosting a team party for a job well done. I've done all of these, many times, and been happy to pay for it out of my own pocket (a necessity in an environment where cuts force out the niceties). Trust and respect are not things you can demand, they have to be earned. If you treat others as you'd like to be treated, with honesty and decency, it tends to come around, especially when it matters most.

Under the old hierarchies, when being a boss was all about consolidating power, there was scant appreciation for developing workplace relationships in this way. But today, when it's not about power but about building connections with employees and the customers you serve, it's the smart way to operate. According to research from Exeter and the Netherlands' University of Groningen, men view influence as an attribute that wins over employees and gains their acceptance, while women view employee acceptance as a factor that leads to influence. In these new ways of working and leading, women have an edge.

It's a Woman's World

RECENTLY, THE NEWS WEBSITE Mashable featured a colourful graph illustrating the way social media is changing how companies have to do business. Taken from data from Soren Gordhamer, author of *Wisdom 2.0*, it highlights how companies have to shift from selling to connecting, from running large campaigns to small acts, from controlling the message to transparency, and from being hard to reach to being available virtually everywhere. What's striking to me is that women usually excel at all the non-traditional ways that a company now has to position itself in the market. Women have already demonstrated, in dramatic fashion, that they are remarkably comfortable communicating and wielding influence in the digital sphere: they dominate the web. Several studies and surveys, from the Pew Research Centre, Nielsen and Burst Media, have found that women are the heaviest users of social media sites—and not just teenage girls, but women ages forty through sixty. They're more likely than men to have a blog or a well-developed digital persona, to share photos and videos, to shop online, to consume news, comment and interact with brands.

I also think that where some women might lack the time to reach out to strangers through old-school, face-to-face networking channels, or feel uncomfortable doing so, they have found in the web a new and liberating way to connect. I'm someone who is generally shy and often runs on a tight schedule; the digital sphere allows even a time-taxed introvert like me to be an extrovert, to engage and network. A *Fast Company* article from February 2015 suggests that introverts are, in fact, the best networkers on Twitter. It featured a marketing manager from Georgia who described herself as "extremely shy" and said that because of social media she had been able to advance professionally much faster and further than if she had been limited to face-to-face events. Even my mother, whose stroke cost her the ability to speak and move, is active online. With nothing more than the slight mobility of a single finger on her right hand, she taps out messages, tweets and loves to post pictures on Throwback Thursdays.

The point is that women can thrive in the information age, as users of the technology and as entrepreneurs. They've been starting an average of more than five hundred companies a day in the last seven years, launching businesses at twice the rate of men, according to a 2014 report from American Express OPEN. Based on data from the US Census Bureau, the report also finds that between 1997 and 2014, the number of women-owned firms grew at one-and-a-half times the national average in the US. If that's not a testament to women's ability to go boldly into this information age, to take risks and lead in volatile times, I don't know what is. Some of this growth can

be explained by an increase in self-employed women benefit-
ing from the flexibility tech provides to better juggle work and
family, as in the rise of the "mompreneurs." But that's only
part of the story. With the exception of large, publicly traded
corporations, the report found that not only revenue, but
employment growth among women-owned firms, topped that
of all other firms. (Remarkable, too, is the double-digit growth
in the number of companies launched by women of colour,
who now own one in three of all firms started by women in
the US.) In all, the report estimates that as of 2014 there were
nearly 9.1 million enterprises owned by women, employing
7.9 million workers and generating $1.4 trillion in revenues.

At the same time that women are branching out on their
own in ever-growing numbers, they are also well placed to
play a leading role in the economic sectors that will matter
most in the coming years. The US Census Bureau estimates
that women make up more than two-thirds of employees in
ten of the fifteen job categories expected to grow most quickly
over the next decade. These categories include health, social
and educational services, but also technical occupations in
accounting, science and law. Meanwhile, women are well
placed to rise through the ranks in their chosen fields as they
continue to acquire the lion's share of post-secondary education. According to Statistics Canada's 2011 National Household
Survey, 55 percent of adults between the ages of 25 to 34 with
a college diploma were women. Women also represented 59
percent of young adults with a university degree, 58 percent
with a master's degree, and 62 percent of adults with a medical degree. The only university-degree level at which young
women are not the majority of holders are doctorates, but

even there women are close to half, obtaining more than 47 percent of PhDs.

Millennial women, some thirty million of them in North America alone, are making their way in the workforce, better educated, more optimistic and more confident than any generation of women before them. They aspire to leadership roles more than their grandmothers and mothers. By some accounts, such as research from the Pew Center, their aspirations still trail those of men. But this cohort of females, from their twenties and into their thirties, is almost as likely as their male counterparts to ask for a raise and a promotion. And more than half of them—61 percent—say they hope one day to be the boss. I suspect they'll have their shot. These Gen Y women have grown up in a digital world. Not only do they naturally possess the skill set that I think modern leaders need, they've already forged a galaxy of connections and built a sphere of influence likely to carry them through the rest of their lives. They have swallowed whole from birth changes that older generations are still struggling to digest. And so, should they choose to, the new generation of women making their way into the workforce by the millions has the right stuff to lead in any sector, and conquer any cliff.

IX

Your Turn

WHEN I MOVED MY FAMILY back from Denver to Toronto in the early 2000s, I took my youngest daughter to work with me at Alliance Atlantis one afternoon. The company had a sprawling studio and office set up in a midtown tower and as we stepped onto the elevator, my daughter, who was used to visiting my office at Hallmark, automatically pressed the button for the top floor.

"Nooo," I said. "My office is down here." As I pushed the button for a lower floor, she shot me a look of surprise that basically said, "What's up with that?" (This was the same daughter who, when I announced I was Top 40 Under 40, responded with "Well, what number are you?" Tough audience.) In her mind, I would be on the top floor because I was the boss. But at Alliance Atlantis, I was "back a step" and I was good with that. My job put me on the creative side of the table and it was a position that made me happy, no matter what floor my office was on.

It's natural to think you haven't made it until you reach the top of your field. But what's truer today than ever before is that the dispersal of power within business means you don't have to be the boss to be a leader. And "having it all" could mean staying for a while at a job that makes you happy. What's key to feeling successful is drawing satisfaction from the contributions you make at whatever level you choose to work. A career worth having is not about collecting titles, but about the experience you get along the way. Yes, I went from girl Friday to president before I was thirty, but the thread that runs through my career is not straight up. Leading involves the ability to inspire others to contribute, but to do that, I think you first have to be inspired yourself. I may have found natural footing in the higher levels of management, but if those responsibilities took me too far away from involvement in creative content—searching for it, developing it, promoting it—I lost interest. That's what motivated me. I know that when my interest dwindles so does my desire, and my ability, to contribute. That's why I left behind the president title at Paragon and why, after having a more senior job at Hallmark, I chose to work lower down the corporate ladder at Alliance Atlantis. The substance of the work I was doing always mattered more to me than status and title, and that, ultimately, is why I also left the top job at the CBC.

I was barely two years into my tenure as executive vice-president when the leader's ledge had shrunk to a razor's edge at the public broadcaster. The deep budget cuts that came in 2012 suddenly made my job more about balance-sheet management than creative leadership. It also meant that there was little chance of good work being rewarded. There was talk of innovation, but no resources to invest in it. I didn't slip from a glass cliff, I looked over the edge into an unfair future and I walked away. It wasn't a difficult decision. I love exploring new possibilities in the media world: I was there at the dawn of cable programming, and the advent of digital offerings too. Joining Twitter, and starting a new business for them, gave me an opening into the tech world that's completely redefining how we produce and consume content. It's not one-way broadcast, it's a multidirectional platform upon which anyone can contribute, create and share. I left a narrowing place for a wide-open playing field.

If we're honest with ourselves, I think we all know what drives our happiness. But it's what we do with that knowledge that can make all the difference. Through the course of your career, you need to keep asking yourself whether you are satisfied. What makes you satisfied can change radically with experience and with age. Do you have a position that allows you to contribute in ways that matter to you right now? Do you feel your talents are well applied? What is success to you? Is it personal growth, money, recognition? If you feel successful then you are successful—and you are where you are meant to be. If you don't, then change is the answer.

But change comes in many forms. It might mean you move to a new firm, or take on a different job in your existing organization, vie for a more senior role or switch jobs completely. No one, especially not me, has all the answers. There's no one size that fits us all when it comes to decisions in the personal or professional sphere. What I ask is that you consider what "getting ahead" means to you, and that you don't let pressures from others or society as a whole dictate what success looks like to you. We spend enough time at work that we need to spend that time being happy with what we do and how we do it. If you want to advance your career by taking on more responsibility at work, then feel free to look for it, ask for it; let your higher-ups know when you're ready to take on bigger challenges, and be clear about what you want. And get ready to work hard.

To distinguish yourself as a leader you need to show that your goals align with the company's trajectory. That you can harness the resources, and, when needed, build a team you can empower and motivate to help you achieve success. To stand out as a valuable member of the team you have to make sure you understand what you're playing for and that you can see the big picture. Educate yourself about the aims and needs of your organization and then work strategically to meet them.

Back at Alliance Atlantis, for instance, I knew the lifestyle channels needed a shakeup and I'd seen the trends in the US toward dramatic storytelling over the traditional how-to, and its potential to resonate with audiences. I also knew that Canada was desperately short on its star-making system, and here was this completely unplowed field of talent in a genre that was just taking off. And so I forged a plan, and then shared my thinking with the team of how we might build the audience and the network's brand by developing our own homegrown celebrities. It paid off, but it was about taking a chance to do something in my department that would be of benefit to the organization overall. If you can make your outfit look good or make the life of your boss easier, your efforts will be noticed.

This all factored into the strategy that earned me my first major promotion at Paragon, although, at the time, I'm not sure I recognized it as a strategy. Isme Bennie received dozens of calls in a day and I thought, "Why not do more than take a message? Why not do more to help?" I'd overheard enough of her conversations to know which questions to ask. So I tried them out: "What type of content are you interested in? Who is your audience? Here's a few of the shows we have that might work for you and here's why." I had no inkling that my boss was within earshot, sizing me up. All I knew was that I was hungry for bigger challenges than answering phones and sending faxes. And I was determined to prove that I could handle more, to myself as much as anyone.

Stepping up and showing initiative is the most concrete way for anyone to demonstrate that they are all in, a true team player with an understanding and willingness to move the puck up the ice. At every place I've worked, the employees I value most are the ones who come to me and say, "I was thinking that it might be worth approaching such and such this way." People who recognize problems but approach me about them ready to offer solutions hold a special place on my teams. These are the kinds of gestures that can help build your personal capital. And, down the road, that can pay huge dividends.

It's in You to Give

PERSONAL CAPITAL IS YOUR CURRENCY. It's what you build and use when you put yourself up for a new role, suggest a way forward or successfully present an idea—especially an unpopular one. (You know the stakes are high when you're willing to risk your personal capital to back a strategy with opinion stacked against it.) Personal capital is tied to your authority, credibility and reputation. It represents the total value of your professional experience, your network, knowledge and know-how, your wins and all that you've learned from your losses. The only way to make more of it is to spend it wisely. The more expertise and experience you accumulate, the more chances you take and the more initiative you show, the more capital you stand to earn and the more you have to spend. And you *have to* spend it. In that way, at least, it's not like money—personal capital earns no interest just sitting in your account.

Not long after I became executive VP at CBC, I had to make a call about how much of mine I was willing to gamble. Despite four years in charge of television programming I'd never had much to do with the production of *Hockey Night in Canada*, far and away CBC's most popular and lucrative show. Richard Stursberg had overseen that area personally and, together with the sports department, ran a fairly closed shop. Hockey was, after all, Canada's game, and *Hockey Night in Canada* quite possibly the most "Canadian show of all time," as one pundit put it. That meant there were rules around the way things were done, and you didn't mess with the rules. Only after I replaced Richard did I have my first look inside the world he had fiercely protected. And what I saw was a show in danger of becoming stale, that had been produced and executed in the same style for years, largely by a group of white guys. A fresh approach was overdue. For starters, our audience wasn't just a bunch of white-guy sports fanatics. Families watched—I watched, as did other women, men and kids of all colours. If we were going to offer the

NHL a reason to keep airing its games on the public broadcaster, then the CBC had to demonstrate that we knew how
to leverage our cultural significance to give the games a broad
viewer base—certainly broader than the hard-core male fans
that dominated the sports audiences of private networks.

The first thing I did was put a woman in charge of production at *HNIC*, a clear signal of a new direction. Julie Bristow
was a great production leader, and she brought in Andi Petrillo
as a host and reporter, the show's first full-time female staff
member, and Kevin Weekes, a former NHL goalie and already
a star on the NHL Network, joined the desk. I put Jeffrey
Orridge in charge of managing the CBC's relationship with
the NHL. (Orridge, a New York–born lawyer, has since been
named the first African-American commissioner of the
Canadian Football League—in fact, the first African-American
commissioner of any pro sports league in North America.)
Making the changes was not an easy sell. I was a newcomer to
a precious realm, and a woman amongst men (mostly). But my
job was made easier because of the track record I had to trade
on: I'd spearheaded changes to CBC television that had helped
to increase ratings and revenues and make great shows.

I'd put my personal capital to work, but that was just the
start of the spending spree. *HNIC*'s future at the CBC was
about to face its greatest threat. The NHL broadcast rights
contract was less than three years away from renewal and
things didn't look good. Broadcast licensing fees were skyrocketing as TV execs saw the prize in capturing rapt audiences in real time when so many viewers were slipping away
to watch DVDs or stuff on the Internet or were dumping TV
altogether. For their part, the sports staff at CBC were fiercely

proud and some even felt that the brand of *Hockey Night in Canada* was more important to Canadians than the NHL's. By the time I took over, the relationship between the CBC and the NHL had been strained to the point that it seemed no matter what money we brought to the table, Commissioner Gary Bettman would be just as happy to take his games someplace else.

I needed to do something to fix this, and I drew on my love of another sport entirely. I'd been a long-time fan of the National Football League, and during the season, from Thursday through to *Monday Night Football*, I watched all the games I could. I watched not just as a football fan but as a TV exec who admired the way CBS and NBC produced their broadcasts. Along with a catchy opening number from the likes of Faith Hill or Carrie Underwood, every game started with, "This is a presentation of the NFL," with its logo looming large. But *Hockey Night in Canada* didn't lead any of its broadcasts by stressing that NHL connection. No one makes changes to *HNIC* lightly, but I made a call and said its time we showed the NHL we are their partners, and are invested in growing their brand in the same way we are interested in growing ours.

That season the NHL shield shone brightly beside our *HNIC* logo and on air we reinforced what I had told Gary Bettman we would do going forward: we weren't the partners with the biggest chequebook, but we would be the ones who invested in their brand alongside ours. In sports, teamwork is respected: the NHL noticed this first step of many we then took in working together to bring Canadians the best of hockey.

My years spent partnering with broadcasters, distributors, production companies and studios of all sorts and sizes convinced me that success is built on mutual respect and a commitment to strive to meet each other's goals. Good relationships start with a thorough understanding of what it is your partner values the most. At Paragon, my first sales job involved selling programming to the Middle East. One of our most popular and profitable programs at the time was *The Raccoons*, a children's cartoon series we'd sold into the UK, Australia, Germany and France. Broadcasters in the Middle East wanted it, too, and were ready to buy the hit show sight unseen, even though it didn't come cheaply, given there were sixty-five episodes, at a cost to them of tens of thousands of dollars each. But I had to tell them right off the top that the show was not for them because the foils to the friendly raccoons were dastardly pig characters. And in the Middle East, pigs—good or bad—are censored on TV out of respect for the Islamic religions of the region. I could have made the deal and made my commissions. But it likely would have been the last thing I sold them. Instead I said no, and my grateful partners thanked me profusely and bought three other series that suited their schedules. Asides from those revenues, I gained their trust.

In the case of the NHL and Gary Bettman, we needed to assess what was in it for them to stay with the CBC as we got closer to the looming hockey licence expiry. We'd gotten back the Olympics, but the NHL rights in Canada are the holy grail for broadcasters. Bell and Rogers could offer integrated options with access to their cable and cellular assets. And they had much deeper pockets. Our chance to stay in

the game was to show the NHL how we valued their partnership and their brand, and to show the benefit to them of *our*
assets: a venerable brand in *HNIC*; access through our local
stations to communities across the country to build the rele-
vance of hockey; the talented production staff and on-air per-
sonalities who had produced an amazing show for years; our
ability to feed content out on radio and online. This was not
the kind of direct benefit cash would bring, though we did
have some of that to spend too.

Then, all too suddenly, we didn't. After the budget cuts,
we were hard pressed even to be at the bargaining table, let
alone be a significant player. I left my job soon after rolling
out the leading edge of the major cuts, hoping that the good-
will we had built meant the NHL wasn't going to take their
puck and go home. Sure enough Rogers came with an offer
the NHL couldn't refuse. But the CBC sports production team
got to play an important role in the new *HNIC*, which also
stayed on the network, though in a different form. And the
friendship and collegiality I'd developed with Gary Bettman
carried through to my job at Twitter; he vouched for me in my
new role and our teams now work together, bringing Twitter's
video platform and other innovations to the NHL.

I think too often women underestimate the value of their
currency, its power to influence opinion, reshape a relationship or pave the way for new opportunities. Like information,
we can be hesitant to use it, reluctant to call any attention to
our professional successes; it's just not what "good girls"
do. And there's probably nowhere that's more obvious than
in the stubborn gap that still exists between the wages of men
and women.

It's in You to Ask

LAST FALL, IN PHOENIX, ARIZONA, where more than seven thousand female engineers had gathered for an international conference for women in computing, Microsoft CEO Satya Nadella stepped in it big time in an onstage interview with Maria Klawe, a board member of Microsoft. When she asked him what advice he would give to women who are "uncomfortable asking for a raise," he responded: "It's not really about asking for the raise, but knowing and having faith that the system will actually give you the right raises as you go along. And that, I think, might be one of the additional superpowers that, quite frankly, women who don't ask for a raise have, because that's good karma. It'll come back."

Unfortunately, you can't take karma to the bank and faith has been a lousy provider. According to 2014 figures from the US Census Bureau, the system currently pays American working women about 78 percent of what men make. In Canada the gap is slightly narrower, with 2015 data from Statistics Canada showing that women earn 82 cents for each dollar a man earns. But when you include the weekly wages of part-time workers in 2014, the wage gap widens: Canadian women make about 75 cents for every dollar a man makes. And this disparity persists even in fields like nursing, where women outnumber men by ten to one. A recent study in the *Journal of the American Medical Association* found male nurses outearn their female colleagues by more than $7,000 per year in outpatient settings and close to $4,000 in hospitals.

Nearly everywhere I've worked, I've inevitably tripped over the gender wage gap, with women earning less than their male peers and men earning more than female colleagues with more responsibility—myself included. More than once I have been promoted only to discover that the men who reported to me made more money than I did. The notion that pay raises will simply come to those who wait has all the credibility of the Tooth Fairy. It's no wonder Nadella's comments sparked an instant backlash online. Nadella, to his credit, backtracked immediately and apologized for his answer, admitting he was "completely wrong." In an internal memo he wrote, "I believe men and women should get equal pay for equal work . . . If you think you deserve a raise, you should just ask."

But there's the rub. Not enough women do ask. Granted, the gender wage gap is a complicated problem. Women are more likely than men to interrupt careers to care for children and never quite catch up on the pay scale if and when they jump back into the workforce. Women are also more likely to turn down higher-paying promotions, due, at least in part, to family demands. And, of course, the ugly vestiges of sexism are still at work, even in the West, where we'd like to believe gender discrimination is dying. Even after you take into account that women often work in different fields than men, or that they have different work experience, education and union status, 41 percent of the gender wage gap is still un-explained, according to the Georgetown University Center on Education and the Workforce. In an essay called "Gender Discrimination is at the Heart of the Wage Gap" published in *Time* last May, the center's director, Anthony P. Carnevale and his co-author Nicole Smith, a professor at the center, argued that when social scientists control for every employment factor that could possibly explain the disparity, women still earn only 91 percent of what men earn for doing the same job. But just as there are still patriarchal perspectives to be toppled, women also have a role to play in closing the wage gap. The very fact that Maria Klawe's question pointed out that women can be uncomfortable asking for a raise is evidence of that. We have to ask ourselves, *why* are we uncomfortable?

On one hand, I think we're often so grateful—thanking our lucky stars—that we nabbed the job, we forget that wishing on a star didn't get it for us: we earned it. If you're feeling grateful, the last thing you're inclined to do is ask for more. Good girls get what they deserve and they don't make a fuss or challenge authority. Too often, women fear that they will be seen as pushy or ungrateful, or worse, unlikeable, if they do, and plenty of research backs them up. All this might explain why so many women who know they *should* negotiate simply don't. The Levo League, for instance, a social network that helps Gen Y women advance their careers, surveyed 10,000 of its members and found that 95 percent of these women had never asked for anything in their careers: no responsibility, no mentorship, no raise. As well, in research conducted for her book *Women Don't Ask*, Carnegie Mellon economist Linda Babcock found that in a study of MBA graduates, 57 percent of men negotiated the job offer they received, but only 7 percent of women did. Not negotiating when you believe you deserve more is not only a personal loss for you, as an individual, but for wage equality across the organization.

Still, even when we do suspect we should ask for more, we're often unsure of what "more" means: we don't have an accurate sense of our value. Studies consistently find that even before launching a career, men see themselves making more money than women expect to earn. A recent feature in *The Atlantic*, for example, included the view of Marilyn Davidson, a professor at Manchester Business School in England, who each year for seven years has asked her students what they expect to earn, and what they deserve to earn, five years after graduation. Every year she finds "massive differences" between the male and female responses: On average, men think they deserve $80,000 a year and the women $64,000—20 percent less. A 2014 Columbia University study featured in *Business Insider* found that high-ability women in college expect to earn 31 percent less than men expect to earn at age 30, and 39 percent less at age 45. It's a disparity that can be partly explained by the fact that men are 82 percent more likely to major in business and seek jobs in the higher-paying fields of finance and economics, while women are 62 percent more likely to major in the humanities, which typically pay less. But the study found that even within those fields the gap persists, which can be attributed in part to the fact that men were twice as likely as women to overestimate their true ability level. Call it the expectation gap, but it seems to be one only made wider by the gender gap in confidence. Even in Hollywood, an industry of multi-million-dollar paycheques negotiated by lawyers and agents, it seems to be alive and kicking.

Last fall's infamous hacking of documents and emails at Sony Pictures revealed that male actors were paid significantly more than female actors working in the same movie, most notably, in *American Hustle*. Actors Christian Bale, Bradley Cooper and Jeremy Renner all received a significantly larger share of the profits for their roles in the Oscar-nominated film than their female co-stars Amy Adams and Jennifer Lawrence. When asked to explain the pay gap, departing Sony executive Amy Pascal said during an interview at the Women in the World conference in February 2015 that the women, or their agents, didn't ask for more. "I run a business. People want to work for less money, I'll pay them less money. I don't call them up and go, 'Can I give you some more?' . . . What women have to do is not work for less money. They have to walk away. People shouldn't be so grateful for jobs . . . People should know what they're worth and say no."

And that answer is likely not much different than what would come from any boss minding the purse strings. When women don't ask to be compensated at the same level as men as they start out in their careers, they aren't, and then it's tough to ever catch up. I know this. As a boss, I've seen the disparities, but I also know that trying to correct them is no simple feat. When women and men get the same percentage pay bump for years in a row, the woman never pulls even because she started way behind. As a boss I've never been authorized to spend the money necessary to close the gap once and for all. When raises across the board are limited to a range of 2 to 5 percent a year, there's little room to close that gap. And it is unfair to rob hard-working Peter to pay hard-working Meg.

So how do women close the gap? First of all, we have to ask for that raise. But we have to be smart in how we ask. Too often women have come to me as their boss and tried to justify a raise based on the expenses they face at home: daycare costs, commuting costs, rent, the extra challenges of being a single parent. The trouble with this approach is that your living expenses are your problem, not your boss's. A raise needs to be framed as a recognition of your contributions at work. Salary conversations need to express the idea that compensation-for-work is a value exchange. If you feel you are worth more to your company than you're being paid, or what's been offered, you need to make a business case for why I should spend more on you. So make your request about what you do, about how you make the organization better, about your personal capital and your plans to spend it in order to benefit the firm overall. Keep in mind that a wide range of attributes add to your value as an employee. Do you have a proven ability to form constructive relationships? Do you have the trust of the people you work with? Do they regard your opinion highly? What about your digital presence and profile—do you know how to leverage online interactions in ways that could help the business? All of these are sought-after skills, at all levels, and such skills have never mattered as much as they do now. If you make a strong *business* case to increase your compensation, not only does it convince the boss that you deserve more, it allows the boss to make the case to her higher-ups that it's in their interest to pay you your market value or they will lose you to the market. It won't always work, but if you never ask, you'll never succeed. Make it difficult for me to tell you that you don't deserve the pay you think you're worth. And if your boss does deliver that message, isn't it better to know and make plans to move on to someplace where you are valued?

Closing Gaps While the Windows Are Open

THERE'S BEEN A LOT SAID—and I've already said a lot—about the different ways women and men tend to view success. Often, for women, the perception is that women are less interested in promotions and higher income levels than in personal growth or meaningful work. But I think, in these changing times, there's a growing recognition that these aims are not mutually exclusive and that for women and men the ingredients of success are quite similar. Last summer, for instance, *Forbes* delved into this issue and then carried the results of a survey of four thousand people from the management consulting firm Accenture, which found that both men and women ranked the qualities of career success as work–life balance first, money second, then recognition and autonomy. And a 2010 study in the *Journal of Behavioural Studies in Business* that asked people to define success found that it was men who said "personal growth," while women were more likely to say "career goals."

What's important about this research is that it's a timely reminder that women should not buy into the stereotypical idea that somehow we naturally default to playing supporting roles in the workplace. We have enough barriers to surpass without mistakenly believing that we are all happy with the current scarcity of women in leadership positions.

There's an oft-quoted statistic from an internal Hewlett-Packard study, for instance, that was conducted to figure out how to get more women into management. It reviewed personnel records of employees and discovered that women only applied for promotions when they believed they met

100 percent of the qualifications listed for the job. Men, on the other hand, threw their hat into the ring when they thought they met 60 percent of the criteria. The take-away message has been that men overestimate their potential while women underestimate it, as many other studies have found. But a follow-up study by Tara Sophia Mohr, an author and founder of an international leadership program for women, which was published in August 2014 in the *Harvard Business Review*, found that the application gap really isn't about confidence at all.

Based on a survey of a thousand professional men and women, the study found that the most common reason men and women didn't apply for a certain job was because they assumed the required qualifications were actually *required*, as in: "I didn't think they would hire me since I didn't meet the qualifications, and I didn't want to waste my time and energy." Women were much more likely than men (about 22 percent vs. 13 percent) to say "I didn't want to put myself out there if I was likely to fail." As well, 15 percent of women, versus only 8 percent of men, said they held back simply because "I was following the guidelines about who should apply."

The conclusion is not that women lack the confidence to apply for new positions or promotions, so much as an under-standing of how hiring processes actually work, and that how you sell yourself can trump the hiring criteria. Or as the study put it, "advocacy, relationships, or a creative approach to fram-ing one's expertise could overcome not having the skills and experiences outlined in the job qualifications." In other words, we women are still newcomers to the game and rookies tend to play by the rules. It's no surprise that women would be more inclined to take the job criteria as gospel: girls are raised to follow the rules. Again, in school this wins us awards and degrees, but in the work world it may well limit our careers. But it's not all on female shoulders. As that McKinsey report found, where men are often hired for their potential, women are tapped for their track record. The *HBR* report suggests that this is historical baggage too. Through the twentieth century, at least, women's past on-paper accomplishments, our certificates, diplomas and degrees, *were* our tickets in, proof that we had the credentials to operate in a man's world. But when the world now belongs to us all, when managing out is the new model and influence is the new power, when women increasingly bring the right stuff to drive innovation and success, there's good reason for everyone to fight biases in hiring. All of us need to bring a little more moxie to advocate for ourselves and our ideas—and we need to bring it now.

There's a window opening here and now, and if organizations don't adapt, and women don't act, it can close quickly. The new economy is not without its growing pains. When things are new, they can be confusing and scary, tempting companies old and new to fall back into familiar patterns of hierarchy. Institutions that are struggling to stay in control can be short-sighted. Even young, start-up firms, blossoming with progressive cultures and diverse teams of employees, can be vulnerable to old ways of doing business: the bigger these firms become the more alluring it seems to slip back into old top-down management styles and focus too closely on quarterly results and profit margins. If that happens, organizations can quickly lose sight of the people they serve and the people serving with them.

Pressures from technology and business have combined to make way for a new way of leading, but that will be crushed if we don't move before old biases and habits take hold. And they're never very far away. In March 2015, for example, the *Harvard Business Review* ran a report examining the infamous under-representation of women in science, technology, engineering and math. Other research has suggested the problem is the pipeline, with too few women interested in these territories, or that women in these demanding fields opt out to care for their families. But this report, which involved in-depth interviews with 60 women in science, along with 556 surveys of women in these areas, discovered, once again, that assumptions are dangerous. Women aren't opting out: bad treatment and stereotypical old biases are driving them out. Women in the study said they had to provide more evidence of their competence than their male colleagues, and provide it again and again—especially if they'd had children. They reported that they were expected to fit into stereotypical roles as either office mother or dutiful daughter, at the same time as they had to walk a tightrope between being seen to be too feminine to do the job or too masculine to be liked. Half the respondents reported experiencing a backlash for speaking their minds directly or being decisive.

I can relate to that. Having worked in male-dominated environments, I understand how those feelings of isolation can take hold. Many times I've offered my input or opinion in a meeting—too often as the only woman in the room—to be met with dead silence, which signalled that what I had to say was of so little value it didn't even merit a response. I learned that it helped to align with a male in the group, to say, for instance, "I'm with Steve about this, and I also think . . ." By picking Steve out from the herd, I helped to turn the herd in another direction, or at least pushed them to recognize that there was another direction.

What was also troubling about the Harvard study was that it found that some women reported cold treatment from older female colleagues, who acted as if they were determined to put the younger ones through the same hellish baptism they'd suffered when they started their careers. It was as if these older women believed there still weren't enough positions for women to go around and they had to protect their turf. Yet, as we all know, that's just not the case. There may be particular fields where progress on equal opportunity is still poor, but the days of treating women as mere tokens in the workplace are long gone, given that the kinds of attributes women bring are now crucial elements of success. To create a truly healthy, innovative and profitable culture there has to be more than one or two women at the table. And the more women there are, the more women can connect with one another to advocate for women's interests. We need to see ourselves as strong in the ways that now matter most, and exercise our voice, individually and together.

Our Time

THERE'S MORE VALUE IN being a woman in business today than perhaps ever before. That simple fact should make all women proud; increasingly it's women who are standing out as those with the right stuff to lead. The way in which business is quickly transforming has created many opportunities for women to step up as leaders and put our best selves forward. We are leaving the old ways behind, which is good because it was those old ways that created inequality. It's our turn to forge new ways of working and leading.

I wanted to write this book because I've experienced it all. I started at the bottom, with no connections and no real credentials, and now I'm here. On the way, I had wins but I also had misses, and I suffered through many moments when I was tempted to second-guess myself or fold to stale opinions and old ways of doing things. But I'd like to think that my ongoing story illustrates that success follows when you stay true to yourself.

There was nothing rarefied about my path to success. Mine was a modest childhood, and my professional start was just about as modest as it gets. But I was always aware of my strengths. I knew what engaged me, consistently kept an eye on significant trends and was prepared to take advantage of the opportunities that came my way. In some cases, I fell into a new path, as with Twitter. In others, when it felt like something was the perfect next step, I made an effort to get the job. But, from my first position as a girl Friday on, I believed that I could meet the challenge ahead and took advantage of any smart opportunity. I hope that my story says to girls and young women like my own daughters: "If she can do it, so can I."

As a title I chose simply: *Our Turn*. No subtitle to qualify that claim. I think this is *the* moment for women to see themselves for the leaders they can be. The digital world has made traits associated with interpersonal skills and emotional intelligence into business assets. Those qualities, once labelled and dismissed as "feminine," are crucial to the collaborative, speak-up cultures businesses need to create today in order to survive and thrive. It takes discipline, diligence and practice to recognize such assets and build on such strengths. I confess that sometimes I would watch *The Devil Wears Prada* and wish for just one minute that I could behave as recklessly as Miranda Priestly did. What if just once I could make outrageous demands and show the world who was boss? Wouldn't it be simpler if I could throw my weight and new-found power around and not worry about the consequences? But if you throw your power around today, you might as well throw it out the window. Being an effective leader takes a lot of focus, not on your own needs, but on the needs of others. It takes dedication to something larger than yourself. Technology has made our huge world tiny. It's made every voice matter and given every voice a way to be heard. It's turned influence into the new power, and the act of building pathways, inside and outside our organizations, the best way to channel it. And that's good news, not bad: these days, every person can use their personal capital without being chained to a desk. Going forward, the pressure is only going to mount on employers to make workplace participation and flexibility standard features if they want to keep their talent and stay competitive. Ideas, not objects, fuel the knowledge economy, which means that talented people are the true powerhouses of business.

The ideal is to tap into the knowledge economy to build a team you trust, who manage their own time, tackle tasks in their own way and exert greater control over their own schedule. Technology has given us the tools to make all that possible. In today's market, the idea of finding a good employment "fit" goes two ways. You should spend as much effort as your company spends in making sure you are right for the job, and even more on ensuring the environment is one where you will thrive. A happy life is not about striking that elusive work–life balance, but managing the flow.

Increasingly, men are looking for that same flexibility in their careers. On the home front and the work front, the roles of men and women, fathers and mothers, are slowly converging. More women are becoming the breadwinners, more men are raising children, families are changing their fundamentals in lots of different ways, and the shift is all part of a wider social revolution propelled by the up-and-coming generation of digital natives.

Change is all around us. Our ability to communicate, consume and access information at high speeds has transformed the way we live, work and play, turning our universe into a world of customization, whether it's the music we select for our playlists, the shows we download, the unpackaged holidays we plan or the way we structure our working hours. Today's whatever, whenever, however reality has created utter upheaval in the market, breaking old business models as customers, not bosses, wield the clout that can make you a winner or a loser. Is this change intimidating? Absolutely. But it's exhilarating, too, if only for the horizons it has blown wide open. It's time to get past the bogged-down debates about how women can force change in the workplace and capitalize on the dazzling changes already afoot.

Those glass cliffs have become pinnacles from which new styles of leading can evolve. Women, who have had to struggle for position in a world that only paid them lip service, are perfectly placed to dig in their heels and stand tall.

[ACKNOWLEDGEMENTS]

One day, after giving a speech to a room full of inquisitive and energetic women, a man came out of the crowd and asked me if I'd considered writing a book. "Oh no," I immediately responded. I'd seen books written by various men who had held the jobs I had held. "I have no intention of writing about my time at the CBC." I couldn't imagine anything less interesting to read, let alone to write.

"No, not that story," said the man who became my literary agent, Chris Bucci, who has guided me through to the launch of this book. The story he wanted me to write was about my experiences as a woman and leader in business today. I'd talked about my journey in life and in my career in the speech he'd just heard, and he thought that my optimistic take on the shifting tides of business and how they were creating opportunities for new leaders like myself was a story people would like to hear. By complete surprise it turned out a few editors agreed with him. I soon found myself at a diner sitting across the table from one in particular, Anne Collins, whose well-earned reputation for being one of the best in the business I found slightly intimidating. But we immediately connected over shared stories of challenging career paths with steps taken forward, sideways and back again and the lessons learned in between, and then we bonded over our discussion of "having it all" and what that meant for women in today's world. Anne, and her colleagues at that first meeting, Kristin Cochrane and Brad Martin, thought that my notion that this is the best time for women and for those of us who choose to lead differently than how we once were led, was the kind of message that would inspire others to take up the charge.

I confess that I set out to write this book certain that my English-literature degree meant that the ideas would just flow—I mean how hard could it be for a woman who loved words and ideas to write a book? Well that was another lesson I quickly learned. As you just read, I learned long ago that even when you are championing your own best ideas, you can't be expert in everything it takes to execute them. Successful leaders know what they don't know and they fill those gaps with the most talented people they can find. And after meeting Chris and teaming up with Anne, I was lucky to partner with a wonderful writer, Carolyn Abraham, who brought my ideas and the stories of my journey together in a way I could never have accomplished on my own. Carolyn sat with me for hours of interviews over the course of a year, and put up with a multitude of late night emails from around the world as I attempted to answer her probing questions. Carolyn, a distinguished science journalist and the author of her own insightful memoir, *The Juggler's Children: A Journey into Family, Legend and the Genes that Bind Us*, bonded with me over shared stories of juggling family and career, laughed with me over mistakes we'd both made that proved to be valuable life lessons and got riled up with me over the injustices and unfairness that too many women face as they pursue their careers. Carolyn's careful crafting, together with hours of research by Beth Brudjn to add flesh to my ideas where they needed it, and Anne's superstar edits combined to make the book in front of you. (And thanks to Chris for timely prodding, too.) I pride myself on my ability to build great teams, and this experience, far removed from the daily trials of my work life, proved to be one of the most satisfying for me yet.

[INDEX]

KIRSTINE STEWART oversees Twitter's North American media partnerships across all vertical channels, including television, sports, music and news. Previously, she served as managing director for Twitter Canada, leading Canadian operations and advertising business and partnerships. Prior to joining Twitter in May 2013, Stewart was the executive vice-president of CBC's English services, CBC/Radio-Canada, where she oversaw the network's English-language radio, television and digital operations. Earlier, she was senior vice-president of programming for Alliance Atlantis, overseeing HGTV, Food Network, National Geographic, BBC Canada and others. Stewart earned a bachelor's degree from the University of Toronto, and is a graduate of the Global Leadership in the 21st Century program at Harvard University's Kennedy School of Government. She is @kirstinestewart on Twitter.